ZOOLOGY

AN INTRODUCTION
TO THE ANIMAL KINGDOM

BY

R. WILL BURNETT
Professor of Science Education,
University of Illinois

HARVEY I. FISHER
Chairman, Department of Zoology,
Southern Illinois University

AND

HERBERT S. ZIM

Illustrated by
JAMES GORDON IRVING

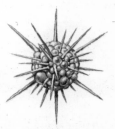

A GOLDEN SCIENCE GUIDE

GOLDEN PRESS · NEW YORK

Foreword

This book introduces a new series—the Golden Science Guides—concerned with exploring major ideas or areas of knowledge. Zoology, the science of animal life, is one of these great areas of knowledge of tremendous importance to us. Not only have the ideas of zoology challenged man's thinking about himself and his place in the world, but facts about animals have been of great practical value. Better health, more food, improved clothing and scores of industrial improvements stem from applications of zoological knowledge. We hope that this book will open the way for your further study and enjoyment of animals. A companion volume, soon to be published, deals in a comparable fashion with botany, the science of plant life.

R. W. B.
H. I. F.
H. S. Z.

LIBRARY OF CONGRESS CATALOG CARD NUMBER: 61-8328
SEVENTH PRINTING, 1962

CONTENTS

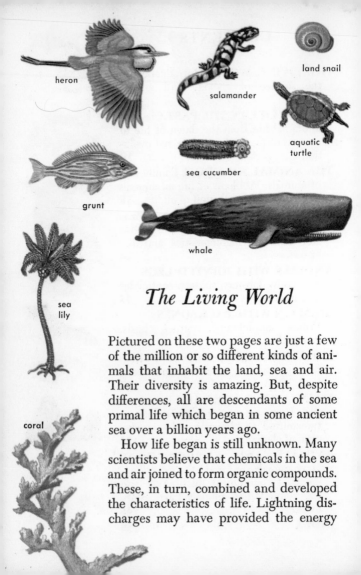

heron

salamander

land snail

aquatic turtle

sea cucumber

grunt

whale

sea lily

coral

The Living World

Pictured on these two pages are just a few of the million or so different kinds of animals that inhabit the land, sea and air. Their diversity is amazing. But, despite differences, all are descendants of some primal life which began in some ancient sea over a billion years ago.

How life began is still unknown. Many scientists believe that chemicals in the sea and air joined to form organic compounds. These, in turn, combined and developed the characteristics of life. Lightning discharges may have provided the energy

boll weevil

butterfly

grasshopper

iguana

platypus

starfish

spider

cuttlefish

mandrill

for this reaction—so some recent experiments suggest.

The ancient ancestor of modern plants and animals must have been extremely simple. It probably used chemicals from the sea for energy and growth just as some bacteria do today. And, most important of all, it reproduced—the first link in the great chain of life.

But conditions changed on the earth. Seas dried up, mountains became plains, and plains became seas. As the earth changed, so did the life upon it. Simple primal life spread through the seas and developed into the plants and animals which later were able to live on land.

jellyfish

mammals

birds

reptiles

leeches

VERTEBRATES

amphibians

bony fishes

protochordates

ECHINODERMS

sharks

sea lilies

starfishes

sea urchins

sea cucumbers

comb jellies

brittle stars

CTENOPHORA

COELENTERATES

sponges

corals

jellyfishes

hydrozoans

SPONGE

THE ANIMAL WORLD can be shown as a tree.
The base of the trunk represents unknown, primitive
forms of life from which all plants and animals arose.
Branches represent main groups or *phyla*. Each

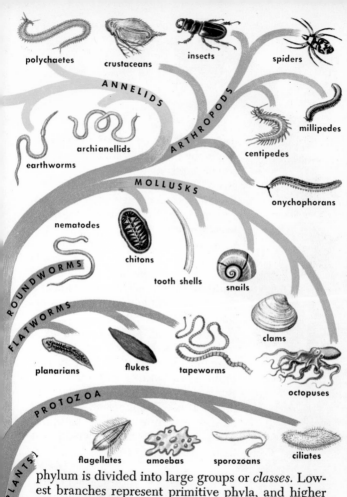

polychaetes

crustaceans

insects

spiders

ANNELIDS

ARTHROPODS

millipedes

archianellids

centipedes

earthworms

MOLLUSKS

onychophorans

nematodes

chitons

tooth shells

snails

ROUNDWORMS

FLATWORMS

clams

planarians

flukes

tapeworms

octopuses

PROTOZOA

(PLANTS)

flagellates

amoebas

sporozoans

ciliates

phylum is divided into large groups or *classes*. Lowest branches represent primitive phyla, and higher branches the more complex groups. These groups of animals are described from pages 24 through 96.

Malarial parasite—
the smallest animal

Goby—½ in.—
smallest vertebrate

Man—about mid-
point in size in
animal kingdom

Elephant—the
largest living
land animal

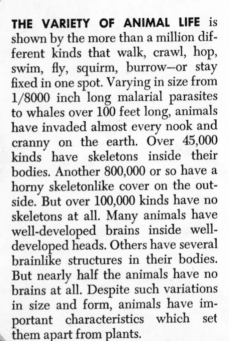

Blue whale—
the largest
animal of any kind

THE VARIETY OF ANIMAL LIFE is shown by the more than a million different kinds that walk, crawl, hop, swim, fly, squirm, burrow—or stay fixed in one spot. Varying in size from 1/8000 inch long malarial parasites to whales over 100 feet long, animals have invaded almost every nook and cranny on the earth. Over 45,000 kinds have skeletons inside their bodies. Another 800,000 or so have a horny skeletonlike cover on the outside. But over 100,000 kinds have no skeletons at all. Many animals have well-developed brains inside well-developed heads. Others have several brainlike structures in their bodies. But nearly half the animals have no brains at all. Despite such variations in size and form, animals have important characteristics which set them apart from plants.

WHAT IS AN ANIMAL?

All animals feed on other animals or plants. Plants make their own food—from carbon dioxide, water and other simple chemicals.

Animals generally move about freely. Most plants are fixed in one place; only a few simple kinds can move about by swimming.

Most animals have a nervous system and react quickly to disturbances. No plant has a nervous system and most respond slowly.

Growth occurs in nearly all parts of the animal body; it slows or ceases at maturity. Higher plants grow only at tips and in girth. Plant growth continues throughout life.

Animal cells are within thin, delicate membranes and lack heavy supporting walls. Most plant cells have thick self-supporting cellulose walls.

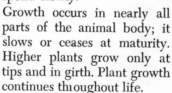

Flagellates make food as plants do and move as animals do. They have both plant and animal characteristics. What are they? Botanists say plants; zoologists say animals.

Animal Life of the Past

The first evidence of life is found in rocks laid down approximately a billion years ago. By the time of the Cambrian period in geologic time (chart, p. 16), about four hundred million years later, a wide variety of jellyfishes, echinoderms, mollusks, worms and crustaceans had evolved. More recent rocks contain fossils showing progressively greater diversity and complexity.

Fossil records of changes in some animal forms are remarkably complete. The chart below gives evidence of changes in the forefeet and skulls of horses. The pages that follow show reconstructions based on fossils. They illustrate the changes which have occured since the dawn of life—changes which continue even today.

Fossils show evolution of modern horse from Eohippus

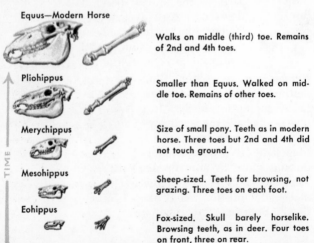

Equus—Modern Horse

Walks on middle (third) toe. Remains of 2nd and 4th toes.

Pliohippus

Smaller than Equus. Walked on middle toe. Remains of other toes.

Merychippus

Size of small pony. Teeth as in modern horse. Three toes but 2nd and 4th did not touch ground.

Mesohippus

Sheep-sized. Teeth for browsing, not grazing. Three toes on each foot.

Eohippus

Fox-sized. Skull barely horselike. Browsing teeth, as in deer. Four toes on front, three on rear.

TIME

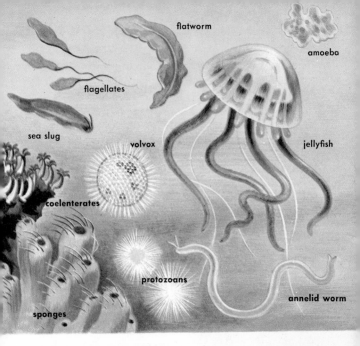

flatwom

amoeba

flagellates

sea slug

volvox

jellyfish

coelenterates

protozoans

annelid worm

sponges

THE DAWN OF LIFE doubtless occurred over a billion years ago in an ancient sea by some chance combination of simple materials. The first speck of life probably had no cellular structure; it may have been similar to present viruses. These can reproduce themselves but have characteristics of nonliving as well as living things. The picture above is an imaginary presentation of the types of animals that lived a thousand million years ago. But it depicts life which had already evolved over millions of years from the first bits of living stuff. Being soft-bodied, few of these ancient animals left direct fossil remains.

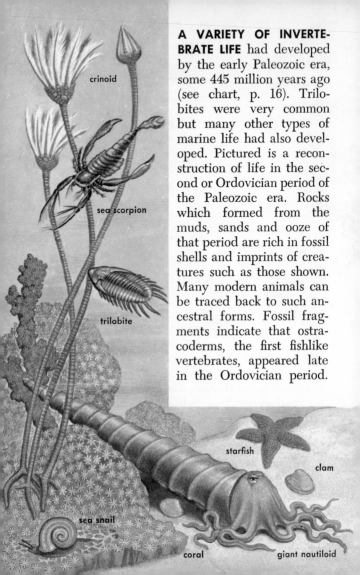

A VARIETY OF INVERTE-BRATE LIFE had developed by the early Paleozoic era, some 445 million years ago (see chart, p. 16). Trilobites were very common but many other types of marine life had also developed. Pictured is a reconstruction of life in the second or Ordovician period of the Paleozoic era. Rocks which formed from the muds, sands and ooze of that period are rich in fossil shells and imprints of creatures such as those shown. Many modern animals can be traced back to such ancestral forms. Fossil fragments indicate that ostracoderms, the first fishlike vertebrates, appeared late in the Ordovician period.

crinoid

sea scorpion

trilobite

starfish

clam

sea snail

coral

giant nautiloid

Lungfishes (Eusthenopteron) leaving the water

VERTEBRATES BECAME COMMON later in the Pale-ozoic era. By the Silurian period (375 million years ago) primitive fishes and sharks had appeared. By Devonian times (350 million years ago) fishes were widely distributed and varied. During the Devonian period lungfishes (p. 69) developed. These had swim bladders connected with the throat so that they could breathe air. Some of these crept onto the shore, as shown above. Their probable amphibian descendents of the late Paleozoic are shown below. By the end of the Paleozoic, land-dwelling insects, amphibia and reptiles all had appeared.

Amphibians (Diplovertebron)—probably descendants of lungfishes

Pteranodon

Brontosaurus

Tyrannosaurus

THE AGE OF REPTILES—the Mesozoic era—which began about 200 million years ago, was a time when reptiles were abundant. Early in this era, small dinosaurs and the first mammals appeared. Later, primitive toothed birds and more mammals developed. Throughout the Mesozoic era, the dinosaurs (meaning "terrible reptiles") and other reptiles were dominant. The giant genra such as Brontosaurus and Tyrannosaurus lived toward the end of the Mesozoic era. At that time, Pterodactyls (flying reptiles) flew through the air and large marine reptiles swam the seas.

Tetonius

Uintatherium

Eohippus

Paramys

Hyrachyus

THE AGE OF MAMMALS—the Cenozoic era—began about 70 million years ago and continued into the present time. The mammals of the Mesozoic era were small and unarmored, but they were intelligent, and very active compared to the dinosaurs. By the beginning of the Cenozoic era mammals had evolved into a variety of forms and sizes. The great spurt of mammal development occurred during the middle of the Cenozoic era. Some of these mammals were large, odd shaped, with unusual body structures. Shown above are mammals of that time—some of which have left modern descendants.

			Millions Years ago
CENOZOIC	Recent	Modern mammals and man dominant. Great Lakes appeared as glaciers melted.	.01
	Pleistocene	Stone age cave men. Mammoths and gigantic mammals. Repeated glaciation.	1
	Pliocene	Elephants, horses, other mammals more like modern types. Climates cooling.	11
	Miocene	Modern meat-eating mammals appear. Mammals widespread. Climates mild.	26
	Oligocene	Higher mammals evolving rapidly. Alps and other mountains rising.	36
	Eocene	Many primitive mammals disappear and modern orders appear.	55
	Paleocene	Rise of placental mammals and modern birds. Considerable mountain building.	70
MESOZOIC	Cretaceous	Toothed birds, first snakes, modern fishes. Dinosaurs die out. Cool climates.	130
	Jurassic	Age of dinosaurs. First birds, crocodiles and lizards appear. Lands swampy.	165
	Triassic	Dinosaurs and bony fishes common. Reptiles dominant. First mammals.	200
PALEOZOIC	Permian	Primitive reptiles become common. Modern insects develop. Mountains form.	230
	Pennsylvanian	First reptiles. Insects common. Amphibians dominant. Warm climates.	250
	Mississippian	Insects increasingly common. Amphibians developing rapidly. Land swampy.	280
	Devonian	Fishes widespread. Amphibians appear. First crabs. Seas spread over continents.	350
	Silurian	Scorpions and spiders become first air-breathers. Invertebrates widespread.	375
	Ordovician	Primitive chordates. Invertebrates evolve. Seas cover most of North America.	445
	Cambrian	Invertebrates only. Abundant shelled animals; no land animals. Mild climates.	550

DEVELOPMENT OF ANIMAL LIFE

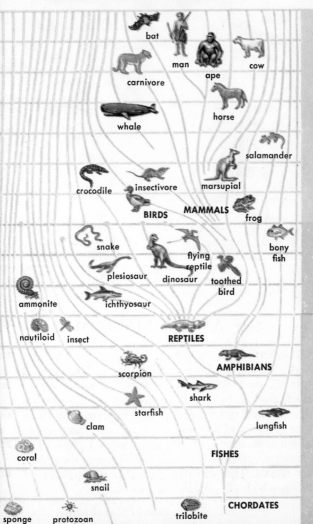

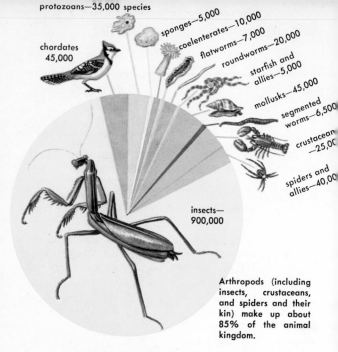

protozoans—35,000 species

sponges—5,000

coelenterates—10,000

chordates
45,000

flatworms—7,000

roundworms—20,000

starfish and
allies—5,000

mollusks—45,000

segmented
worms—6,500

crustacean
25,00

spiders and
allies—40,00

insects—
900,000

Arthropods (including insects, crustaceans, and spiders and their kin) make up about 85% of the animal kingdom.

THE ANIMAL KINGDOM

Classification shows animal relationships. The animal kingdom has been divided into 10 large groups (phyla), each with broad common characteristics. Each phylum breaks down into classes. Classes are divided into orders; orders into families, and these into genera and species. Above are the approximate number of species in the main animal phyla. The classes of arthropods (by far the largest of the phyla) are shown. The next pages show basic problems of living which all animals must solve.

Single-celled amoeba flows around its food.

Fish (many-celled) has a complex digestive system.

FIVE BASIC PROBLEMS OF LIVING must be successfully solved by all animals if they are to live and reproduce. The tremendous variety of animal life in the world today has resulted from the continual attempts of animals to solve these problems in an ever-changing environment. Some descendants of the first simple animals changed with their environments. When changes aided them in dealing with their basic life problems, they lived and had offspring. When changes were unsuccessful, they died.

1 Getting food into body cells is the first problem. Several life processes are involved. For most animals the problem is twofold: food must first be obtained and then brought into the body (above); then it must be changed or digested and transported (below) to every cell. A variety of organs help animals in these tasks.

In complex organisms, the blood carries food and oxygen to all cells.

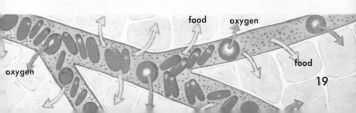

food   oxygen

oxygen

food

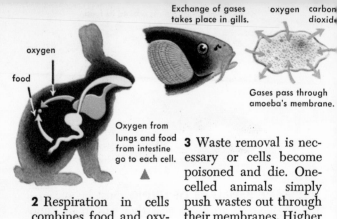

Exchange of gases takes place in gills.

oxygen carbon dioxide

Gases pass through amoeba's membrane.

oxygen

food

Oxygen from lungs and food from intestine go to each cell.

2 Respiration in cells combines food and oxygen to produce energy and wastes. Energy is essential for all life processes. Man's lungs, fishes' gills and the moist skins of earthworms and frogs help absorb oxygen. A variety of hearts, blood cells and vessels transport oxygen and food to all the body cells.

3 Waste removal is necessary or cells become poisoned and die. One-celled animals simply push wastes out through their membranes. Higher animals require complex organs which, together with circulatory systems, help move wastes from all the cells to outside their bodies.

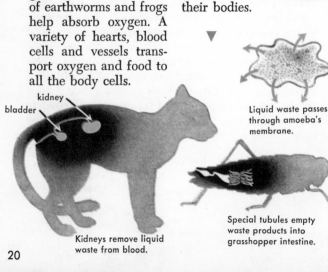

kidney

bladder

Kidneys remove liquid waste from blood.

Liquid waste passes through amoeba's membrane.

Special tubules empty waste products into grasshopper intestine.

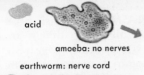

acid

amoeba: no nerves

earthworm: nerve cord

hydra: nerve net

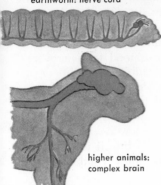

higher animals: complex brain

4 One-celled animals move toward or away from stimuli. Multicellular animals respond as a whole and millions of cells take part. The basic life characteristic of sensitivity or irritability is involved in everything we do.

5 Reproduction makes it possible for an animal *species* or kind to continue after the individual dies. One-celled animals simply split to become two. Sexual reproduction occurs in nearly all animal groups and is most complex in the higher animals. Reproduction is as vital to the species as the other life processes are to the individual.

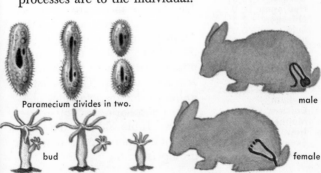

Paramecium divides in two.

bud

Hydra reproduce sexually or by budding.

male

female

Higher animals reproduce sexually.

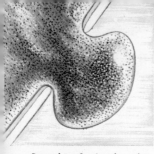

Protoplasm flowing through microscopic opening.

PROTOPLASM, the stuff of life, is made mainly of:
Proteins
Carbohydrates
Fats
Salts
Water

Its average chemical composition is:

Oxygen	76.0%
Carbon	10.5
Hydrogen	10.0
Nitrogen	2.5
Sulfur	0.2
Phosphorus	0.3
Potassium	0.3
Chlorine	0.1

Less than 0.1%
Sodium
Calcium
Magnesium
Iron
Several other elements.

PROTOPLASM is the basic stuff of which all living things are made. It is typically a grayish, slimy material containing tiny particles. It grows by absorbing foods and changing them chemically into more protoplasm. It also burns food for energy and always exhibits irritability or sensitivity. Protoplasm is made of some of the same chemical elements found in nonliving things; yet it is endowed with the unique qualities of life. It is an exceedingly complex combination of chemicals.

Proteins are the most common organic substances in animal protoplasm. They contain nitrogen, carbon, hydrogen, oxygen, usually sulphur, and traces of other elements. Protoplasm also contains sugars, starches and fats. These substances are made of carbon, hydrogen and oxygen. Animal protoplasm is from 50 to 90% water. Most of the common mineral salts found in sea water are also present. These contain sodium, calcium, potassium, chlorine, phosphorus and other elements. Table salt is the most common mineral to be found in protoplasm.

CELLS are the building blocks of all life. Even single-celled animals are usually quite complex and exhibit all the basic life processes. Multicellular animal cells are both complex and highly specialized. Nerve cells, long and thin, conduct electro-chemical impulses. Muscle cells contract. Some blood cells act like independent animals in the body. Disc-shaped red blood cells carry oxygen. Glandular cells produce many different chemicals; bone cells secrete tough or hard material in which they are imbedded. But whatever their shape or special function, all cells are basically alike.

nerve cell

muscle cells

white and red blood cells

bone cells

gland cells

fat cells

covering cells

ANIMAL CELL

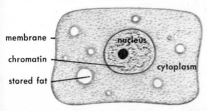

membrane
chromatin
stored fat
nucleus
cytoplasm

Protoplasm of a typical cell includes a covering membrane and a nucleus that is necessary for growth and reproduction. Chromatin in the nucleus sets the hereditary pattern. The rest of the protoplasm, cytoplasm, is responsible for the other life processes. In it are spaces or vacuoles containing foods, wastes or other substances.

Radiolarian—a marine protozoan

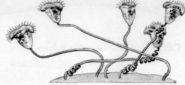
Vorticella—a fresh-water protozoan

Lower Animals

Protozoa, sponges, corals, worms, clams and starfish are the most ancient of modern animals. But they are not simple, either in structure or habits. The one-celled protozoa, for example, carry on all the complex living processes of higher animals.

Protozoa—meaning "first animals"—are found almost everywhere. A quart of stagnant pond water may contain millions. Thousands teem in a bit of garden soil. As spores, some survive dryness for months, then begin to grow again when conditions are favorable. Some are parasites of animals, including man. More than 35,000 species of protozoa are known. Though single-celled, they show many specialized structures. Some have "eye spots" sensitive to light. A few manufacture food as plants do (p. 26).

Spore of heliospora— a protozoan parasite

All can reproduce asexually by dividing and becoming two animals. Some protozoa secrete shells of silica or lime. Some form colonies which function like a single multicellular animal. Some, like Volvox (p. 27) form colonies in which certain individuals specialize in reproduction, others in food-getting, and so forth.

Amoeba causing dysentery

Trypanosome of sleeping sickness

Plasmodium causing malaria

PROTOZOAN KILLERS cause serious diseases of man and animals; amoebic dysentery, African sleeping sickness and malaria are examples. Malaria, caused by a plasmodium, is carried by the Anopheles mosquito (see below). Injected with the mosquito's saliva, the amoeba-like sporozoites enter red blood cells (1). Each forms spores (2), which multiply, then break out (3) at regular intervals, causing chills and fever each time. Some spores develop into sexual forms (4), which the mosquito takes in when it bites an infected person. In the mosquito's stomach these form eggs (5) and sperms (6). Each fertilized egg (7) develops in a capsule (8) in which many new sporozoites form. These migrate to the salivary glands (9), and are injected as the mosquito bites.

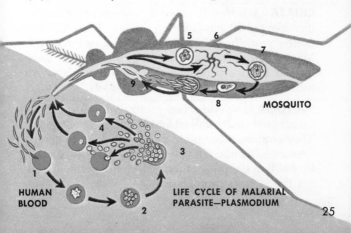

MOSQUITO

HUMAN BLOOD

LIFE CYCLE OF MALARIAL PARASITE—PLASMODIUM

MASTIGOPHORA—the flagellates—have one or more whip-like flagella for movement. Some, like the colonial Volvox, contain chlorophyll and make their own food. Gonyaulax causes the "red tide" which destroys fishes, poisons mussels and causes the seas to glow at night. A related form makes "red snow."

SARCODINA, also called Rhizopoda, are amoebas which move by pseudopodia—temporary extensions of protoplasm from any part of the cell. Some, like Difflugia, have delicate "skeletons" of silica; others, like foraminifera, form shells of lime. Some of the Sarcodina are parasitic.

SPOROZOA are all parasitic and cause diseases of animals. They are usually not mobile and lack structures found in other protozoans. Their life cycles involve an alternation of generations marked by a sexual stage followed by an asexual stage with reproduction by simple division.

CILIATA or Infusoria move by means of cilia—tiny hair-like projections covering the cell. These wave in unison propelling the animal forward or backward. Most ciliates are free swimming; Stentor and some stalked species remain anchored in one place. All use cilia to whip food into their "gullets."

SUCTORIA have cilia when young. Adult forms (pictured) are usually stalked and live fixed in one place. They capture other protozoans with long fingerlike "tentacles." Some tentacles are tipped with suckers for holding the prey; others, which are pointed, suck out the victim's protoplasm.

Gonyaulax

Volvox

foraminiferan

Difflugia

Coccidium

Porospora

Paramecium

Stentor

Podophyra

Acineta

Venus's flower basket skeleton

simple sponge

bath sponge

SPONGES are permanent colonies of animals with a definate body plan and division of labor. There are no organs like hearts or brains, but the cells form simple tissues and carry on specialized jobs.

The 5000 or more species are grouped into three classes. 1. Calcareous (limy) sponges have spicules (spiny, crystal-like structures) of lime embedded between the outer and inner walls. 2. Glass sponges (Venus's-flower-basket, for example) have spicules of silica. They are found in the oceans at depths of 300 feet and more. 3. The largest and most varied class includes the common bath sponge whose flexible skelton (made of spongin) cleaned of protoplasm was once widely used in households. Also in this class are about 200 small freshwater sponges. Sponges pictured above actually live in different habitats.

SPICULES OF LIME

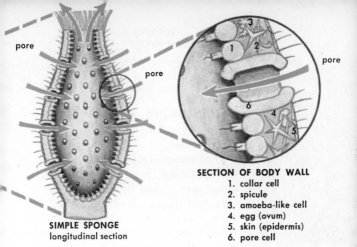

pore

pore

pore

pore

SECTION OF BODY WALL
1. collar cell
2. spicule
3. amoeba-like cell
4. egg (ovum)
5. skin (epidermis)
6. pore cell

SIMPLE SPONGE
longitudinal section

SPONGES have a body wall pierced by tiny pores (from which the phylum name, Porifera, comes). The inner wall is lined with collar cells bearing flagella. These whip water through the pores and out through an opening at the top. Microscopic plants and animals are swept into the collar cells and digested. The soluble food then diffuses to other cells. Between the thin-celled outer covering and the inner wall are spicules, a fluid, and amoeba-like wandering cells which also digest and circulate food. All sponges have this basic structure, but in the more complex forms the walls are folded to form canals.

Reproduction in some is sexual. The fertilized egg becomes a free-swimming larva, attaches itself and grows into an adult. Many sponges reproduce by "buds" which may drop off to form a new colony.

SPICULES OF SILICA

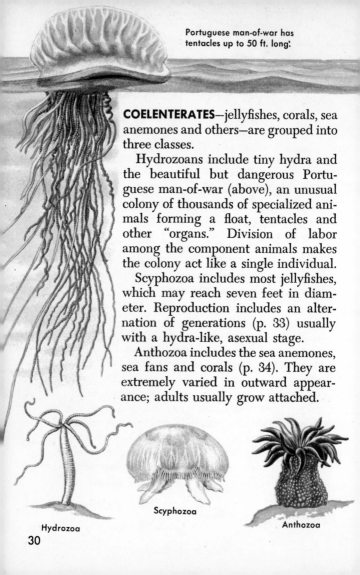

Portuguese man-of-war has tentacles up to 50 ft. long.

COELENTERATES—jellyfishes, corals, sea anemones and others—are grouped into three classes.

Hydrozoans include tiny hydra and the beautiful but dangerous Portuguese man-of-war (above), an unusual colony of thousands of specialized animals forming a float, tentacles and other "organs." Division of labor among the component animals makes the colony act like a single individual.

Scyphozoa includes most jellyfishes, which may reach seven feet in diameter. Reproduction includes an alternation of generations (p. 33) usually with a hydra-like, asexual stage.

Anthozoa includes the sea anemones, sea fans and corals (p. 34). They are extremely varied in outward appearance; adults usually grow attached.

Hydrozoa

Scyphozoa

Anthozoa

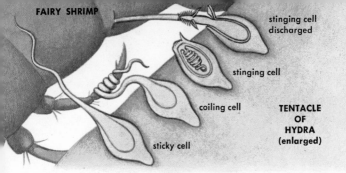

FAIRY SHRIMP

stinging cell
discharged

stinging cell

coiling cell

sticky cell

TENTACLE OF HYDRA
(enlarged)

NEMATOCYSTS are specialized food-getting and protective structures on the tentacles of coelenterates. The coiled nematocysts shoot out when triggered by pressure. The barbed tips of one type penetrate the prey; then a paralyzing poison is injected. Swimmers have been seriously stung by nematocysts on tentacles of Portuguese men-of-war. Another type of nematocyst coils around the victim. A third type sticks to anything it touches.

The basic body plan of coelenterates (below) illustrates the similarity between the fixed polyp stage which is essentially an upturned cup, and the free-swimming medusa or jellyfish stage which is an inverted cup. Many coelenterates alternate between the polyp (asexual) and the medusa (sexual) stage.

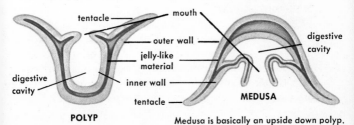

tentacle — mouth

outer wall

jelly-like material

inner wall

digestive cavity

tentacle

digestive cavity

MEDUSA

POLYP

Medusa is basically an upside down polyp.

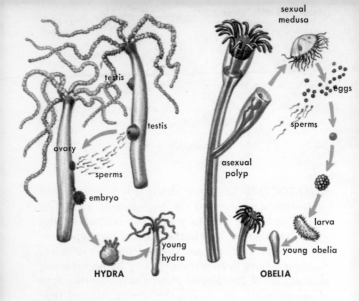

COELENTERATE LIFE CYCLES are pictured above. The chief differences are in the presence, and the size, of a free-swimming medusa which reproduces sexually. The small fresh-water hydra reproduces sexually, and also asexually by budding. It is a hermaphrodite, one animal producing both sperm and eggs. Fertilized eggs grow directly into new polyps without an intervening medusa stage.

Obelia, a tiny marine form, has both a fixed polyp and a free-swimming medusa stage. Obelia is a colonial animal with branching stalks which bear specialized feeding and reproductive polyps. Saucerlike buds break out of the reproductive polyps and swim away to form male and female medusae.

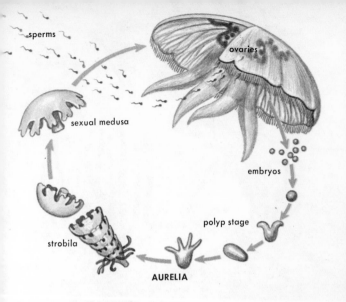

sperms

ovaries

sexual medusa

embryos

polyp stage

strobila

AURELIA

The medusa deposits eggs and sperms in the water. The fertilized egg develops into a free-swimming larva which finally fastens itself to some object, develops a mouth and tentacles, and becomes a fixed polyp. After a period of growth, this tiny polyp produces the new, branched colony by budding.

In Aurelia, the common ocean jellyfish, the free-swimming medusa (3 to 12 inches in diameter) is the dominant and most familiar stage in the life cycle. The fixed polyp which is the dominant stage in Obelia is absent or greatly reduced in size. Fertilized eggs may or may not form a polyp. When they do, the polyp buds tiny medusae which become sexual adults.

staghorn coral

sea fan

sea whip

star coral

brain coral

CORAL ANIMALS are famed reef-builders. Each is a tiny, plump polyp with short tentacles, living in a cuplike limy case which it builds up as it grows. Some corals live as individuals, but most are colonial. The colonies thrive in warm, shallow water—at temperatures above 70°F and at depths of less than 120 ft.—as in the West Indies and in the Indian and South Pacific oceans. Living coral reefs form marine communities with many types of fishes, invertebrates and seaweeds, adapted to life on and around the coral. The colors of the living coral are varied and often brilliant. Exposed coral reefs and coral islands provide land on which millions of people now live.

astrangia coral

Precious coral is made into jewelry. Polyps of coral feed on microscopic life.

CORAL ROCK is built by coral animals, but algae, worms, shellfish, and other creatures live together here in a mutually beneficial association. Some of these other animals and plants also deposit lime.

Coral reefs may be formed in several ways. Darwin suggested that coral first grows along the shore of a mountain peak jutting up through the warm sea, to form a fringing reef. If the mountain sank slowly, the growing edge of the coral would be separated from the island and a lagoon would form between it and the island. Such barrier reefs are known. Finally, if the island was completely submerged only the ring of coral, an atoll, would remain.

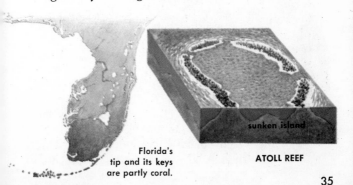

Florida's tip and its keys are partly coral.

sunken island

ATOLL REEF

35

LIFE HISTORY OF LIVER FLUKE

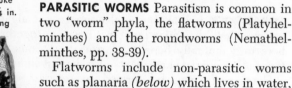

liver
fluke
¾ in.
long

PARASITIC WORMS Parasitism is common in two "worm" phyla, the flatworms (Platyhelminthes) and the roundworms (Nemathelminthes, pp. 38-39).

Flatworms include non-parasitic worms such as planaria (*below*) which lives in water, and parasitic flukes and tapeworms. The human liverfluke infects over 75% of the people in parts of Japan, China, and South Asia. The adult fluke, about ¾ inch long, lives in the bile ducts of the liver; its eggs (1) pass from the body in the feces. The eggs, containing larvae, are eaten by water snails (2) and then develop into another form which passes into the water. They then bore into the bodies of fishes (3). When raw fish is eaten (4)—as is common in the Orient—the young worms swim from the intestine into the fine branches of the bile duct and grow to maturity.

Blood flukes with similar life histories infest blood vessels of animals and humans in parts of Africa and the Orient. A related fluke larva burrows into the skin causing "swimmer's itch," making swimming almost impossible in some lakes of the North Central States.

planaria
½ in. long

36

Tapeworms are marvelously adapted to a parasitic existence inside intestines. They are highly specialized with no digestive tract (they live on food digested by the host) and only rudimentary nervous, muscular and excretory systems. However, their reproductive system is very elaborate. Each tapeworm produces both sperms and eggs.

The beef tapeworm, a parasite of man, has a head with sucking discs which aid the worm in hanging to the intestine wall. Then follow many sections, all alike, which absorb food and produce myriads of sperms and eggs. Matured sections, gorged with fertilized eggs and embryos break off and pass out with the feces. Cattle may pick them up when grazing. If so, the tiny six-hooked larvae are liberated from the old section walls and bore through the cow's intestines to enter the blood. They move into the cow's muscles and there form cysts (bladder worms). If uncooked or under-cooked beef containing cysts is eaten by a person, the bladder worm breaks out of the cyst, attaches to the intestine, and develops into a new worm.

TAPEWORM

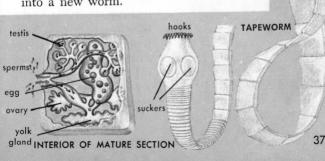

testis

sperms

egg

ovary

yolk gland

hooks

suckers

INTERIOR OF MATURE SECTION

37

ROUNDWORMS (Nemathelminthes) are found almost everywhere. Some are microscopic; one is 14 inches long. A spadeful of rich garden soil may contain millions. "Vinegar eels" and "threadworms" are other examples. But over 50 different species parasitize man and cause such diseases as hookworm, trichinosis and elephantiasis. Few plants or animals are spared. Many crop plants suffer from nematode infections of their roots.

Intestinal Roundworms, of which Ascaris is a common form, infect wild and domestic animals and man. Eggs drop to the ground in animal feces. Humans are infected by eating contaminated food.

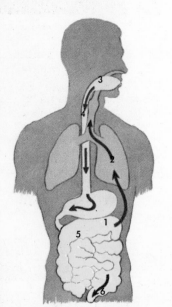

The diagram at left shows the life history of Ascaris. Eggs hatch into larvae in the intestinal tract and bore through intestine wall (1). Blood carries larvae to lungs (2), where they grow. They are then coughed up or crawl up windpipe to back of mouth (3), are swallowed (4), and mature in intestine (5). A female worm living in the intestine may have millions of eggs in its body. These pass out in feces (6) and, if eaten by other animals, start the life cycle over again.

LIFE CYCLE OF INTESTINAL ROUNDWORM

HOOKWORM, once a serious disease in the southern U. S., is still common in the warm areas of the world. Infected people lack energy. The hook-worm life cycle is like that of intestinal roundworms except that infection occurs as larvae hatched in the warm soil bore through the skin, usually on the soles of the feet, to enter the blood.

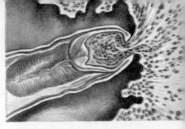

Mouth of hookworm attached to intestinal wall (cross section)

Hookworms mating in intestines (actual size ½ in.)

TRICHINOSIS is caused by the trichina worm, which infects pigs, rats and man. Pigs get the disease by eating infected rats or raw garbage. Man gets it from eating poorly cooked pork which contains larvae in microscopic cysts. Thousands of larvae may be in a single slice of infected pork. The cysts are digested away and the worms reproduce in the human intestines. Larvae then bore through intestine walls into the blood stream. They burrow into muscles all over the body and form cysts. Millions of larvae may be in the body at one time, causing severe pain, weakness and even death.

Trichina cysts in muscle (enlarged)

earthworm

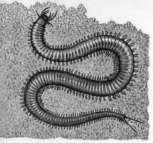
sandworm

pond leech

fanworm

ANNELIDS include earthworms, sandworms, leeches and their relatives. Some live in oceans, some in moist soil and some are parasites. The large size (some 11 ft. long), and the great numbers (over 6000 species) of the annelids make them the most conspicuous of the worms. Earthworms emerge at night to feed on decaying organic matter. They are hermaphrodites. The eggs and sperm are pushed into a mucus sheath which slips over the worm's head and is deposited underground. Bristle feet on each segment help the worm to move.

Sandworms have flattened "paddles" for swimming. Fanworms live in tubes on the sea bottom, waving feathery gills for respiration and for catching small animals. Leeches, found in fresh water and on land in warm moist areas, frequently suck blood.

Starfish feeding on oyster

bulb
sieve plate
canal

INTERIOR TUBE-FEET SYSTEM

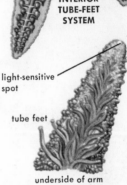

light-sensitive spot

tube feet

underside of arm

ECHINODERMS (spiny-skinned animals) are starfishes, sand dollars, sea urchins, sea lilies and sea cucumbers. The 5000 or so species are all marine. Bodies form a radiating or wheel-shaped pattern (radial symmetry).

Starfishes and some other echinoderms move slowly by tiny tube feet connected to canals filled with sea water. When the bulbs contract, the water extends the tube feet and helps them cling to anything they touch. Starfishes feed on clams; the tube feet attach to the clam shell and the arms slowly pull it open. Then the starfish turns its thin stomach inside out and extends it between the shells, digesting the clam on the spot. Reproduction is sexual; fertilized eggs become mobile larvae.

If a starfish loses arms, it can grow new ones

41

sea urchin

sand dollar test

SEA URCHINS AND SAND-DOLLARS lack arms, but close study reveals the same radial symmetry as in the starfishes. Spines of some tropical sea urchins are poisonous. The jaws have an unusual five-part structure. Sand dollars have shorter spines and tube feet. They feed on bits of organic material. The tests (dried shells) of both animals are often found without spines on beaches.

sea cucumber

SEA CUCUMBERS grow up to 3 ft. in length. Sluggish and leathery-skinned, they feed on organic material in sand. When alarmed they can disgorge internal organs, regenerating a new set later.

SEA LILIES, or crinoids, are stalked echinoderms. The branching rays give a feathery appearance. Widespread 200 million years ago, only one-third as many kinds exist now.

sea lily

bivalves

gastropods

chitons

tusk shells

cephalopods

MOLLUSKS are a diverse group of over 45,000 species, some beautiful, some economically important, some decidedly bizarre. They fall into five classes, illustrated above. Of these, the chitons are most primitive and the tusk shells least common. The bivalves or pelecypods (p. 44) include clams and their kin. The gastropods are the snails, slugs and other single-shelled or shell-less mollusks of sea and land. Cephalopods make up the last class—squid, octopus and chambered nautilus. The octopus, despite its tentacles, horny beak and almost human eyes, has several internal features which relate it to the clam.

Siphons carry water in and out of the clam. Microscopic food is screened out and passes into the mouth. Gills take oxygen from water. A heart circulates blood. The foot is used for movement.

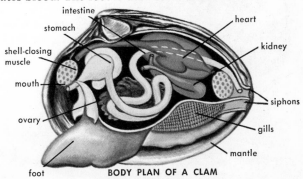

intestine
stomach
heart
shell-closing muscle
kidney
mouth
ovary
siphons
gills
foot
mantle

BODY PLAN OF A CLAM

43

How a clam
burrows into sand

CLAMS, OYSTERS, MUSSELS and many other bivalves (pelecypods) are of economic importance. About 50 million bushels of oysters are sold for food each year in the U.S. alone. Shells of fresh-water clams were once widely used for buttons. The ridges on the shells are growth lines. The great pearl oyster of warm seas is the source of fabulous gems. Pearls develop in this and other bivalves; the thin mantle tissue which lines the shell secretes pearl around irritating grains of sand or parasitic larvae. Like most animals whose young must shift for themselves, bivalves produce vast numbers of eggs.

0
1
2
3
4
yrs.

Lines of growth in a clam shell

A female oyster produces 20 million eggs a year. Oysters grow rapidly. Shell begins to form a day after eggs are fertilized. In three weeks the animal settles to the bottom; it grows rapidly —2 in. in three months.

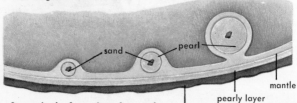

sand — pearl

mantle

pearly layer

outer shell

44 Stages in the formation of a pearl

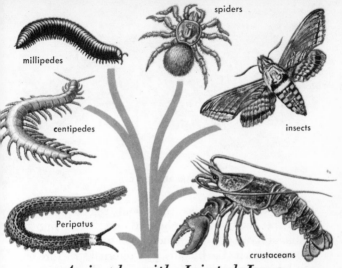

millipedes

spiders

insects

centipedes

Peripatus

crustaceans

Animals with Jointed Legs

Arthropods include insects, spiders, ticks, millipedes, centipedes, and crustacea such as lobsters and shrimps. All have segmented external skeletons (exoskeletons). Over a million species make this the largest and most varied animal phylum.

The arthropod body—as shown in Peripatus, an intermediate form—is similar to that of annelid worms. But the chitin exoskeleton of typical arthropods protects the soft insides and, with attached muscles, makes swift motion possible.

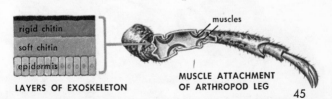

rigid chitin

soft chitin

epidermis

LAYERS OF EXOSKELETON

muscles

MUSCLE ATTACHMENT OF ARTHROPOD LEG

45

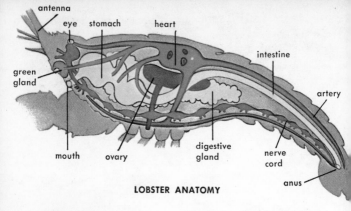

LOBSTER ANATOMY

CRUSTACEANS, a class of about 25,000 species, have the head and the chest (thorax) fused into a cephalothorax. Most of them live in water, mainly in the sea. All breathe by gills. The internal structure of the lobster, typical of crustaceans, is shown above. Horny teeth in its stomach tear food. Kidneylike green glands remove waste. A heart pumps blood into body cavities. After eggs are fertilized they remain attached to the female. Larvae remain attached briefly, then swim away and grow independently.

Lobsters are prized as food. The spiny lobster lacks the large claws. Other edible crustaceans are the shrimps. There are many species—some small ones living in shallow water. The crayfish is a common fresh-water crustacean.

lobster   shrimp   crayfish

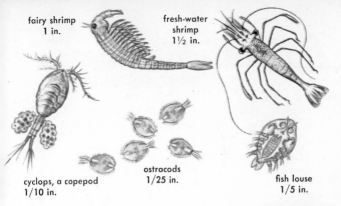

fairy shrimp
1 in.

fresh-water
shrimp
1½ in.

cyclops, a copepod
1/10 in.

ostracods
1/25 in.

fish louse
1/5 in.

SMALLER CRUSTACEANS have greater economic value than the larger forms we use directly as food. The smaller species of crustaceans—especially the copepods—are the principal food of small fishes and are an essential link in the food chain of all aquatic life. Copepods, larvae of barnacles, and other tiny animals and plants are collectively known as plankton. They are abundant in the colder ocean currents and are constantly used as food by fishes.

Barnacles are unusual crustaceans. The larvae are free-swimming, then settle down to become fixed adults with limy plates. In feeding, feathery feet whip plankton into the mouth. Barnacles are usually hermaphrodites, producing eggs and sperm. They grow on piling and foul the bottoms of ships.

rock barnacles

gooseneck
barnacles

hermit crab
out of shell

sow bug

in shell

fiddler crab

ghost crab

OTHER CRUSTACEANS include the sow bug. It is a scavenger, eating plant as well as animal food and is found the world over in moist places. "Beach fleas" (amphipods) live amid the decaying vegetation on all beaches. They are abundant in seaweeds drying at high tide level. Many smaller crustaceans occur by the millions in both fresh water and salt.

CRABS are much like lobsters, but the tail region is greatly reduced and the skeleton over the cephalothorax is large, round and flattened. Hermit crabs use mollusk shells as houses, anchoring themselves with hooklike soft tails. Male fiddler crabs use their huge single claws to entice females in the mating season. Sand-colored ghost crabs are common but difficult to see against the sand.

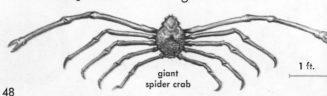

giant
spider crab

1 ft.

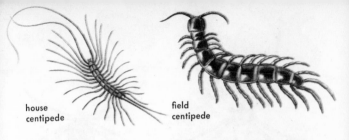

house
centipede

field
centipede

MILLIPEDES AND CENTIPEDES may seem wormlike but their jointed legs, exoskeletons and complex internal structure place them as two distinct classes of arthropods. Centipedes have one pair of legs on each body segment. Small claws attached to the first segment secrete poison, paralyzing prey. The food of centipedes ranges from insects and earthworms to mice and lizards for larger species. About 2000 species are known. The common long-legged house centipede kills insect pests such as cockroaches. Other North American species, found under rocks and stones, are inactive during the day.

The 7000 or so kinds of millipedes have two pairs of tiny legs on each segment. Their class name, Diplopoda, refers to this fact. Some have over 100 segments, thus over 400 legs. These move in a rhythmic, wavelike motion. Millipedes are found in the same places as centipedes, eating decaying organic material or sometimes plant roots. When disturbed they roll up into tight coils, the hard exoskeleton protecting the soft underside.

millipede,
coiled

millipede,
extended

golden orb weaver

young spider parachuting

black widow

SPIDERS and their relatives, the arachnids, differ from insects (pp. 52-64) in having eight legs and a body divided into cephalothorax and abdomen. Spiders usually have eight eyes and mouth parts with poison fangs to paralyze prey. Juices of insects or other animals are sucked as food. Eggs are laid in a silk cocoon and the young look like miniature adults. Not all spiders make webs, but all have spinnerets which make a fine silk thread. Silk is used by different spiders for egg cocoons, webs, traps, for lining burrows, and for wrapping up prey. Newly hatched spiders of some species (called "parachuters") spin long gossamer threads and let the wind carry them. This serves to distribute the young.

The trap-door spider makes a hole in the ground, lines it with silk, and closes it with a hinged lid. Wolf spiders pounce on their prey. Black widow, about ½ in. long and black with a red hour-glass mark on underside, may cause illness and occasionally death with its bite.

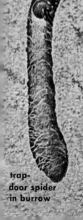
trap-door spider in burrow

OTHER ARACHNIDS

SCORPIONS of tropics and warm climates hide by day, hunt insects and other small animals by night. Sting of tail is painful but in American species is rarely fatal. Young are born alive.

MITES are related to ticks. "Red spiders" feed on plants. Other mites cause certain plant galls and leaf diseases. Chiggers and others burrow into human and animal skins.

TICKS drop from vegetation onto passing animals, pierce the skin and gorge on blood. Rocky Mountain and other fevers are transmitted by feeding ticks. Eggs are laid on the ground.

DADDY LONGLEGS, or harvestmen, are the spiderlike arachnids of fields and buildings. Abdomen is segmented. Food is small insects and organic material.

KING or HORSESHOE CRABS were widespread in ancient seas, but only a few species of this "living fossil" are alive today. Burrowing into sands of shallow waters, it catches sand worms and mollusks with pincerlike legs.

male, ventral view

female, dorsal view

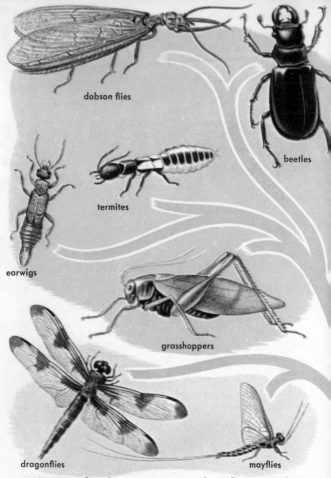

dobson flies

beetles

termites

earwigs

grasshoppers

dragonflies

mayflies

INSECTS, the largest group of arthropods (over 900,000 species) have three pairs of legs, one pair of antennae and usually one or two pairs of wings. The

wasps, bees, ants

fleas

moths, butterflies

flies

caddis flies

sucking lice

bugs

protura

cicadas

body is divided into head, thorax and abdomen. Family tree, above, shows relationship of important orders. Colored backgrounds emphasize kinships.

caterpillar

cocoon

bumblebee   lady beetle   silkworm

IMPORTANCE OF INSECTS is such that it has been suggested that one day insects may inherit the earth. Small size, great variety and a high rate of reproduction have made them highly successful. Many plants require insect pollination to produce fruit and seed. Some insects, like the lady beetle, eat or parasitize harmful insects. Shellac, dyes and even medicines are made from insect bodies.

Insects harmful to man include those which destroy his crops and products. Corn, cotton and wheat have each over a hundred insect pests. Chinch bugs alone do millions of dollars damage annually. Other insects carry diseases, including bubonic plague, typhus, tularemia, malaria and yellow fever. Insects transmit plant diseases, too—as the Dutch elm disease. Finally, some—as lice, fleas and botflies—parasitize man and other animals.

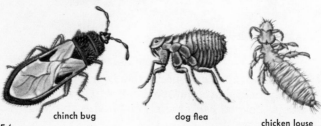

chinch bug   dog flea   chicken louse

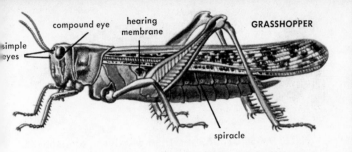

simple eyes · compound eye · hearing membrane · spiracle

INSECT BODY PLANS are much alike. Beside characteristics mentioned on pp. 52 and 53, insects have both simple and compound eyes. In the latter, many lenses form a mosaic image. Breathing is through holes (spiracles) on the abdomen which connect to tubes, or tracheae, and air sacs. These branch into tiny tubes going to body cells. The abdomen contracts rhythmically, forcing air in and out. The grasshopper, a typical insect, has a hearing membrane on each side of the abdomen. Chewed leaves are stored in the crop, ground in the digestive tract, and digested by juices of the digestive gland. Kidneylike tubules excrete wastes into the intestine. The brain and a chain of ganglia on the ventral nerve cord provide nerves for all body parts. The body cavity is filled with colorless blood, pumped slowly by a tubelike heart.

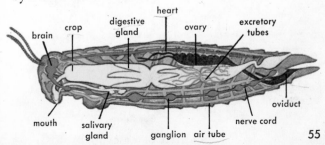

brain · crop · digestive gland · heart · ovary · excretory tubes · oviduct · nerve cord · air tube · ganglion · salivary gland · mouth

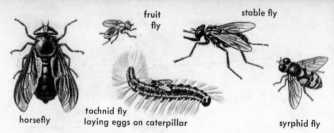

fruit fly

stable fly

tachnid fly
laying eggs on caterpillar

horsefly

syrphid fly

FLIES, MOSQUITOES and their relatives (some 80,000 species) form a group of man's most pestiferous enemies. These insects have one pair of wings and a pair of knobbed balancing organs. Their larvae are wormlike. Adults have biting, sucking or lapping mouths. Flies vary in size from almost invisible midges to inch-long horseflies. Horseflies and stable-flies (which look like houseflies) bite viciously. Houseflies can't bite, but spread germs. The Tach-inid fly and similar forms are parasitic.

Mosquitoes lay eggs on water. Males suck plant juices. Females suck blood. Anopheles mosquito carries malaria (p. 25); Aedes carries yellow fever.

LIFE CYCLE OF HOUSE FLY

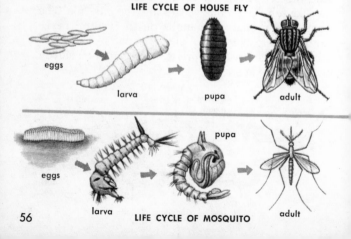

eggs

larva

pupa

adult

eggs

larva

pupa

adult

LIFE CYCLE OF MOSQUITO

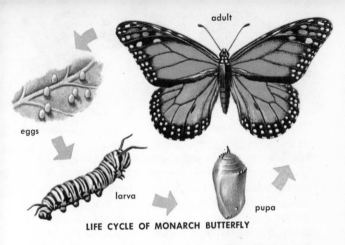

eggs

adult

larva

pupa

LIFE CYCLE OF MONARCH BUTTERFLY

BUTTERFLIES AND MOTHS (over 150,000 species, 12,000 in America) have wings covered with tiny overlapping scales which provide their color. Scales on butterflies are flattened; on moths hairlike. Like flies, these insects go through complete metamorphosis, i.e., four stages of development (egg, larva, pupa, adult). Larvae (caterpillars) of most forms eat plants, and some do great damage to crops —as the codling moth, corn borer and tent caterpillar. The pupa of the butterfly is called a chrysalis. Most moths pupate inside silken cocoons. Strong thread from the silkworm moth cocoon is unwound to make silk. The adult silkworm cannot eat, and lives only long enough to reproduce.

RESTING POSITIONS

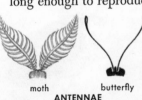

moth   butterfly
ANTENNAE

moth   butterfly

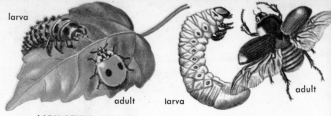

larva

adult   larva

adult

LADY BEETLE—HELPFUL   **JUNEBUG—HARMFUL**

BEETLES are the largest group of insects—more than 277,000 species. Their front wings form a horny sheath which covers a second, folded, thin pair of flying wings. Beetles have chewing mouthparts, and go through complete metamorphosis. Larvae of many species damage plants: the potato beetle and boll weevil are important examples. Fireflies are soft-bodied beetles. The wingless females and most larvae of fireflies (both called glowworms) also produce cold light. Among aquatic beetles are whirligigs—with two pairs of eyes, one pair above the water line, the other below it. Some diving beetles carry air bubbles down with them for an oxygen supply while they are under water.

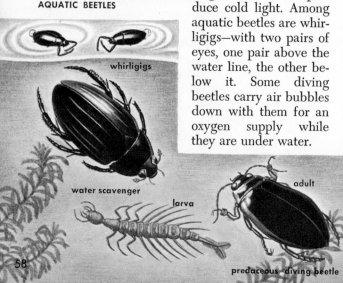

AQUATIC BEETLES

whirligigs

water scavenger

larva

adult

predaceous diving beetle

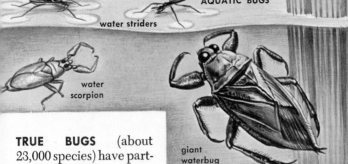

water striders

water scorpion

giant waterbug

backswimmer

TRUE BUGS (about 23,000 species) have partly thickened front wings with membranous tips and piercing-sucking mouthparts. Bugs go through gradual metamorphosis. Their eggs hatch into miniature adults called nymphs. There is no pupal stage. Most bugs suck plant juices—some suck blood. Chinch bugs and squash bugs damage crops. Assassin and ambush bugs are predatory. Bedbugs, a wingless species, live on human or other animal blood. The water strider, back swimmer, giant waterbug and water scorpion are aquatic. Fine hairs on legs of water strider enable it to skate on water. Most aquatic bugs are predators and can inflict painful bites.

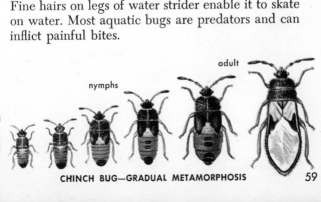

nymphs

adult

CHINCH BUG—GRADUAL METAMORPHOSIS

59

nest

PAPER WASPS

ANTS, BEES AND WASPS (103,000 species), with thin membrane wings, include some insects with elaborate social communities. Most ants live in underground nests with chambers connected by tunnels. Several specialized forms (castes) live in each colony. Males and queen females fly into the air for mating. Queens then shed wings and start new colonies. The most numerous caste is the workers—imperfect females that do the work of the community. Some species of ants stroke plant lice (aphids) and drink the "honeydew" secretion. Others cultivate fungi. One kind feeds some of the workers until they become huge, living storage vats of honey.

PAPER WASPS are also social insects. They chew up wood to build paper-covered nests with one or more tiers of hexagonal cells. Mud wasps are solitary. They paralyze spiders or large insects and place them in mud cells to serve as food for the larvae.

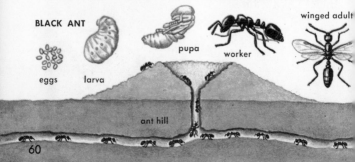

BLACK ANT

eggs

larva

pupa

worker

winged adult

ant hill

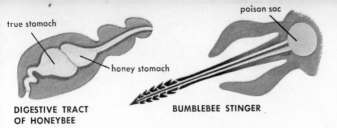

DIGESTIVE TRACT OF HONEYBEE

BUMBLEBEE STINGER

HONEYBEES gather nectar, pollinate flowers, secrete wax and make honey. Honey is made in the honey stomach, found only in workers. Workers are infertile females whose egg-laying organs are modified into stingers. The queen, the only fertile female in the hive, mates but once in her life, storing sperms in her body. Fertilized eggs hatch into workers or queens; unfertilized eggs into males (drones). Larvae are at first fed "royal jelly," secreted by head glands of workers. Worker and drone larvae then receive a mixture of pollen, honey and saliva. Larvae to become queens continue on royal jelly. A new queen bee engages in a mating flight with a drone, then becomes the new hive queen. The old queen "swarms" with thousands from the hive and starts a new colony. Worker bees generally die after stinging, for the barbed sting stays in the wound, pulling the poison sac and other organs out of the bee.

HONEYBEE

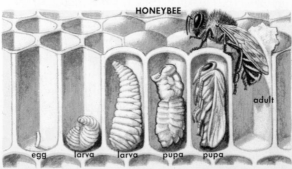

egg   larva   larva   pupa   pupa   adult

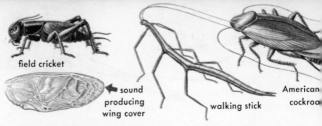

field cricket

sound producing wing cover

walking stick

American cockroach

GRASSHOPPERS, CRICKETS, COCKROACHES and some 22,000 other straight-winged insects have chewing mouths and feed mainly on plants. Eggs hatch into miniature adults called nymphs (gradual metamorphosis). Walking sticks, thin and twiglike, are examples of protective resemblance often found in animals. Male crickets "sing" by rubbing front wings together, or front wings with hind feet.

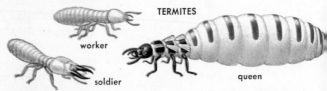

TERMITES

worker

soldier

queen

TERMITES are social insects. Castes include blind workers and pincer-jawed soldiers. Tunneling through wood, they cause great damage. Intestinal protozoa (p. 149) digest the wood termites eat.

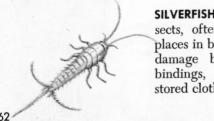

SILVERFISH, primitive insects, often live in damp places in buildings, causing damage by eating book bindings, wallpaper and stored clothing.

DRAGONFLIES and their kin total about 5000 species. They mate while flying. Eggs, laid in water, develop into predatory nymphs. Nymph leaves water, skin splits, and adult emerges. Adults feed on the wing, eating small insects—cannot harm man. Smaller damselflies rest with wings folded.

MAYFLIES appear in great numbers over and near water. Adults live but a day or two, mating in air. Nymphs develop in water, taking several years to reach adult stage. They eat water plants and, in turn, serve as important food for freshwater fish. Adults do not eat. Over 1000 species.

CADDIS FLIES also mate in flight. Females lay eggs in water. Nymphs build protective cases of sand, pebbles, shells or bits of plants and carry these with them as they forage on small water animals. Nymphs are food for fish. About 4500 species.

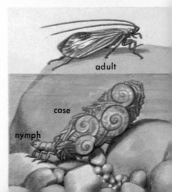

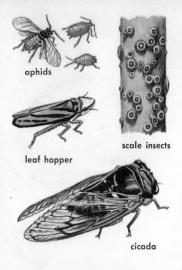

aphids

scale insects

leaf hopper

cicada

APHIDS, LEAF HOPPERS, SCALE INSECTS, CICADAS (about 32,000 species) differ widely in appearance but belong to the same order. Aphids injure plants by sucking their juices. Leaf hoppers may look like thorns. Wingless scale insects suck plant juices under protective scales they secrete. Larvae of cicadas (harvest flies or 17-year locusts) live in the ground. They finally emerge, their backs split open, and adults crawl out and live about a week.

ANT LIONS represent nerve-winged insects. Eggs are laid in sand or loose, dry soil. Larvae, called "doodle bugs," dig pits in sand, lie with jaws exposed, then jostle the sand, causing ants to fall into their waiting jaws.

LICE AND FLEAS, in different orders, are alike in parasitizing man and animals. Lice lack wings. Fleas are wingless, but powerful jumpers.

Ant lion larva trapping ants.

body louse

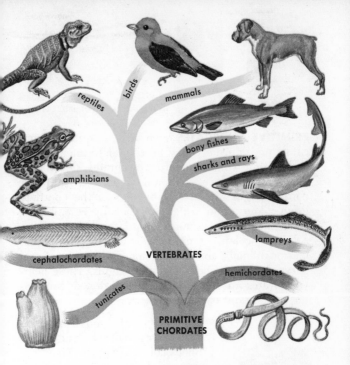

reptiles

birds

mammals

bony fishes

sharks and rays

amphibians

cephalochordates

lampreys

VERTEBRATES

hemichordates

tunicates

PRIMITIVE CHORDATES

Animals with Backbones

Sharks, fishes, amphibians, reptiles, birds, mammals and several minor, primitive groups belong to the phylum Chordata. All have a tubular nerve cord running down the back close to a supporting rod or notochord. All have gill slits at some stage in life. In vertebrates, the embryo notochord is soon replaced by a vertebral column. The family tree above shows the seven classes of vertebrates and the three primitive groups of chordates.

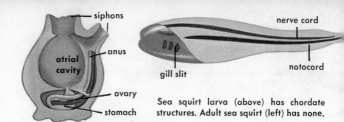

Sea squirt larva (above) has chordate structures. Adult sea squirt (left) has none.

PRIMITIVE CHORDATES such as sea squirts (Tunicates) and lancelets may be similar to ancient animals from which modern vertebrates developed. The sea squirt larva, with a notochord, dorsal nerve cord and gill slits clearly belongs in the chordate group. The adult, which superficially resembles a small sponge, lacks most chordate characteristics. Adult lancelets — Amphioxus (not pictured) — are marine animals, about 2 in. long. They have a dorsal nerve cord, notochord and paired gills. These near-vertebrates are found in shallow water, or burrowing in the sand of beaches.

mouth

LAMPREYS — the most primitive vertebrates—have a true backbone (of cartilage). They use their jawless, circular mouth to attack bony fish. The rasping tongue tears holes in the fish's body. Blood and soft tissues are sucked, weakening or killing the fish. Lampreys are serious pests.

gill slits   **DETAIL OF LAMPREY**   notochord   nerve cord

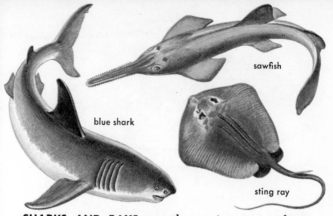

sawfish

blue shark

sting ray

SHARKS AND RAYS, mostly marine, are a large group of primitive vertebrates. They differ from bony fishes in having a cartilaginous skeleton and uncovered gill slits. Shark's skin is rough as sandpaper. It contains many small, pointed, placoid scales. Sharks have row upon row of teeth. These are really large placoid scales, believed to be the forerunner of true teeth. The enamel of all vertebrate teeth develops from epithelial (skin) tissue (pp. 108-109). Rays and skates are similar to sharks but have enlarged pectoral (shoulder) fins, with which they swim gracefully.

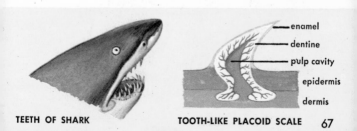

TEETH OF SHARK

enamel
dentine
pulp cavity
epidermis
dermis

TOOTH-LIKE PLACOID SCALE

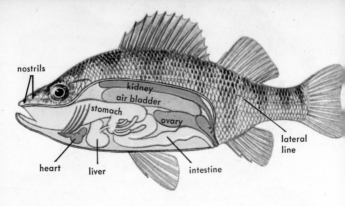

nostrils
kidney
air bladder
stomach
ovary
lateral line
heart
liver
intestine

BONY FISHES are much alike in general body plans (see above). Most are covered with overlapping scales and secrete a slime which reduces friction as they swim. Fish can hear, but have no outer ears or eardrums. A specialized row of pores (the lateral line) on each side serves to detect low frequency vibrations and pressure (p. 104). Nostrils, and taste buds in and around mouth, are extremely sensitive to dissolved substances. Gills (see below) expose miles of thin-walled capillaries to a flow of water from the mouth. Dissolved oxygen is absorbed into the bloodstream and carbon dioxide is given off.

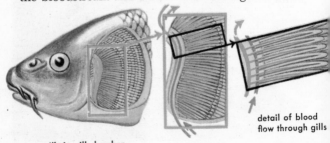

detail of blood flow through gills

gills in gill chamber
(gill cover is cut away)

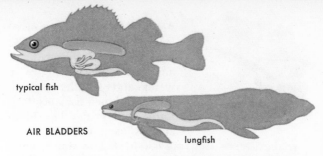

typical fish

AIR BLADDERS

lungfish

The more than 20,000 species of bony fishes have interesting adaptations to the lives they lead. Most fish have an air-bladder which adjusts the fish's buoyancy to pressures at different depths. Lung-fishes have air-bladder "lungs" which open into the throat, as shown above. These aid respiration when the water dries up and may be forerunners of lungs (p. 13). Sea horses swim in a vertical position and wrap tails around water plants. Males shelter the eggs in a brood pouch until they hatch. Deep-sea fishes often produce light (bioluminescence).

sea horse

deep-sea fish

69

tree frog

AMPHIBIANS probably evolved from ancient lungfish (p. 13). The larval forms of frogs, toads and salamanders still live in water and breathe through gills as did their fish ancestors. Later, many develop lungs and assume a part-time terrestrial existence. Eggs are laid in shallow water; males fertilizing them as they are deposited A gelatin layer protects the eggs. Frog and toad tadpoles (larvae) have external gills when young, later internal gills. The tail is slowly absorbed. Hind legs form, then the front legs. Lungs became functional as gills disappear and the young adult develops.

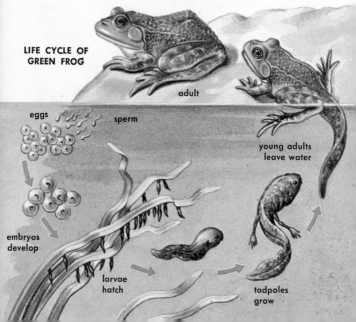

LIFE CYCLE OF
GREEN FROG

adult

eggs

sperm

young adults
leave water

embryos
develop

larvae
hatch

tadpoles
grow

Adults take to the land, but winter in the mud at the bottom of lakes and ponds. Frogs have moist skins which help in respiration (oxygen is absorbed through skin). Toads have dry, warty skins (but do not produce warts). Some

Green frog feeding

salamanders retain their gills as adults. Tongues of toads and frogs are attached at the front and are flipped out to catch insects. Peeping and croaking are the mating calls of males, amplified by expanded vocal sacs. The Surinam toad has divorced itself from water entirely, using fluid-filled pouches on its back as a place for the young to develop.

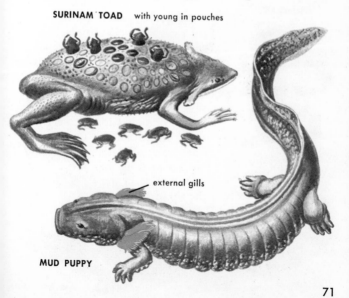

SURINAM TOAD   with young in pouches

← external gills

MUD PUPPY

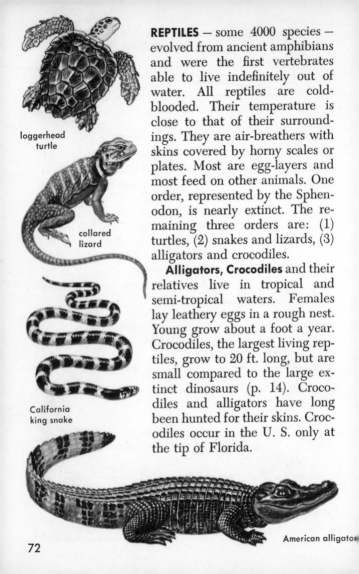

REPTILES — some 4000 species — evolved from ancient amphibians and were the first vertebrates able to live indefinitely out of water. All reptiles are cold-blooded. Their temperature is close to that of their surroundings. They are air-breathers with skins covered by horny scales or plates. Most are egg-layers and most feed on other animals. One order, represented by the Sphenodon, is nearly extinct. The remaining three orders are: (1) turtles, (2) snakes and lizards, (3) alligators and crocodiles.

Alligators, Crocodiles and their relatives live in tropical and semi-tropical waters. Females lay leathery eggs in a rough nest. Young grow about a foot a year. Crocodiles, the largest living reptiles, grow to 20 ft. long, but are small compared to the large extinct dinosaurs (p. 14). Crocodiles and alligators have long been hunted for their skins. Crocodiles occur in the U. S. only at the tip of Florida.

loggerhead turtle

collared lizard

California king snake

American alligator

Common garter snake bears young alive.

Smooth green snake young hatch from eggs.

SNAKES AND LIZARDS are basically similar. Lizards usually have legs and can close their eyes. Snakes have a transparent fused covering over their eyes and are legless. Most snakes and lizards lay eggs. A few kinds keep and hatch the eggs inside the female's body. Both shed their skins as they grow. The Gila monster is the only poisonous lizard in the U.S. Copperheads, moccasins and rattlers are poisonous snakes, with a pit between the eye and the nostril containing cells sensitive to heat. This aids them in striking at warm-blooded animals.

TURTLES, like all reptiles, have lungs, but some can stay under water for a long time. All lay eggs, and even the aquatic species come ashore for this purpose. Turtles have a horny beak instead of teeth. Their upper shell is developed from their ribs. Turtles are long-lived—some surviving for over a century.

Scarlet king snake shedding skin.

air movement over pigeon wing

BIRDS are warm-blooded. Their body temperature stays constant, enabling them to remain active in cold weather instead of becoming inactive as cold-blooded animals must. Insulating fat layers under skin, absent in cold-blooded animals, help maintain body heat. The body is covered with down feathers (see below) which trap air like a warm blanket. Skin muscles automatically fluff heavier feathers to increase thickness of insulation in cold weather.

All birds have feathers. Flight feathers are stiff. Their feathery barbules are interlocked by tiny hooks (barbicels). If barbules are separated, a stroke of the beak (preening) interlocks them again. Feathers are dropped or molted at least once a year and are replaced by new ones. In molting, the bird sheds feathers symmetrically, so that its flight is not disturbed. Molting enables birds to have new, colorful feathers for courtship. Feathers, which are modified scales, are developed from the epidermis.

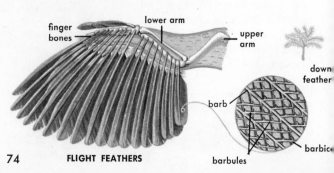

finger bones — lower arm — upper arm

down feather

barb

barbules

barbicel

FLIGHT FEATHERS

BIRD STRUCTURES include many adaptations for flight. The body is streamlined; feathers overlap, lowering air resistance. Wings are set high on a light skeleton. The wing action of birds produces lift for the body for the same reason an airplane wing lifts a plane: the stream of air over wings lowers pressure on tops —so there is relatively greater pressure below. The great flying muscles (white meat of chicken and turkey) are fastened to keel-like breastbone.

When perching birds squat for rest or sleep, knees and heels pull tendons, causing toes to grasp, locking the bird automatically on its perch.

Reproductive system is similar to that of reptilian ancestors. Male has no external organs. Sperms are transferred from male cloaca—into which intestinal wastes and urine also flow—to cloaca of female. Female has only one ovary—the left. Eggs are fertilized in the oviduct, and as they pass down, glands secrete yolk, albumen (egg white) and finally the shell before egg is laid.

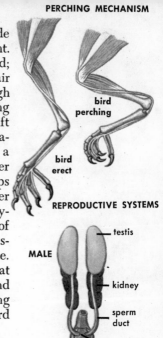

bird
perching

bird
erect

REPRODUCTIVE SYSTEMS

MALE

testis

kidney

sperm
duct

cloaca

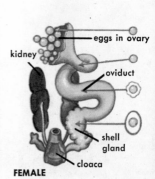

eggs in ovary

kidney

oviduct

shell
gland

cloaca

FEMALE

75

king penguins

kiwi

ostriches

FLIGHTLESS BIRDS, descendants of ancient flying birds, fall into two major groups, the ostriches and the penguins.

Penguins, found in the Antarctic, are webfooted with wings modified into paddles for swimming. They are marine birds, more at home in water than on land. Eggs are incubated by being held on top of either parent's toes.

Ostriches live in the dry plains of Arabia and Africa. They weigh up to 200 lbs. and stand up to 8 ft. high—the largest living birds. They have a 12-foot stride and can run as fast as a horse. Large (4 to 5 lbs.) eggs are laid in a community nest. Other flightless birds are the rhea, cassowary and the long-billed diminutive kiwi, of New Zealand.

SHOREBIRDS AND WATERBIRDS belong to several diverse groups. Waterbirds have oil glands or "powderdown" patches to keep their feathers waterproof. Loons and grebes are expert swimmers and divers, feeding on fish. Ducks, geese and swans have broad, flat bills. They feed on aquatic plants, small fishes and other water life. Most species migrate in great flocks in spring and fall. Herons and cranes are wading birds with long legs, long necks and strong, sharp beaks which they use to catch fish, frogs and crustaceans. Sandpipers, snipes and plovers run along shores catching small animals. Gulls, terns, pelicans and kingfishers also live along the water—each adapted to its own way of life.

tern

loon

gulls

heron

pelican

sandpipers

ducks

PERCHING BIRDS include the common and well-known birds such as the sparrows, warblers, swallows and many other species. All have three toes forward and one behind, an adaptation for perching (p. 75). Many sing melodiously. The windpipe includes a complex sound-producing organ called a syrinx. Nests built by these birds are more intricate than those of most other species.

nuthatches

crows
and jays

titmice

larks

creepers

flycatchers

swallows

FAMILY TREE OF PERCHING BIRDS

tanagers

warblers

finches

vireos

waxwings

blackbirds

kinglets

shrikes

wrens

weaver finches

starlings

thrushes

mocking birds

79

horned owl

BIRDS OF PREY are the larger hunting birds with hooked beaks and sharp talons. They are strong fliers and have keen sight. Actually, the majority of birds prey on animals, from insects and worms to fishes, frogs and mammals. Those commonly called "birds of prey" include eagles, hawks, owls and vultures. The last are scavengers, feeding on carrion. Birds of prey have long been persecuted because a few species occasionally take chickens. But the value of these birds in helping to control rodents and as a check on wildlife populations is now recognized.

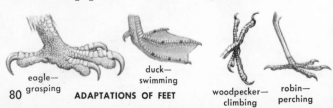

eagle—
grasping

duck—
swimming

woodpecker—
climbing

robin—
perching

ADAPTATIONS OF FEET

eagle—
tearing

sparrow —
seed-cracking

duck—
sieve bill

pelican—
storage

woodpecker— boring

BIRD ADAPTATIONS involve both structures and habits which fit birds to the lives they lead. Such structures are best seen in variations of bills and feet as shown on these pages. The woodpecker, for example, has two toes behind, with which he braces himself as he clings to tree trunks and hammers with his chisel-like bill. Soarers have broad wings; flapping birds, pointed ones. The migration of birds is a functional adaptation involving food and nesting. Some species migrate thousands of miles to and from their nesting grounds. The arctic tern makes a round trip of 20 to 25 thousand miles each year. Birds that do not migrate often develop special habits which enable them to survive the winter. They tend to eat more insects during spring and summer; more fruit or seeds in fall and winter.

Arctic tern migration

81

bat

mouse

squirrel

rabbit

man

ape

RODENTS

scaly-anteater

PRIMATES

armadillo

flying lemur

ground sloth (extinct)

shrew

mole

platypus

opposum

kangaroo

MARSUPIALS

MAMMALS probably descended from flesh-eating reptiles — the Cynodonts. Mammals are the most complex of modern animals. They vary in size from pigmy shrews weighing less than a dime to giant blue whales, over 100 ft. long and weighing more than 110 tons. Most live on or burrow into the land but many live in the sea and some—the bats—have taken to the air. All mammals are warm-blooded, have some hair on their bodies, and suckle their young from mammary glands.

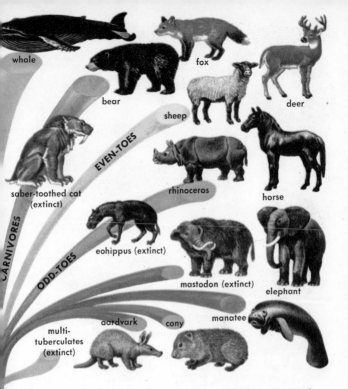

whale

bear

fox

sheep

deer

saber-toothed cat
(extinct)

EVEN-TOES

rhinoceros

horse

CARNIVORES

ODD-TOES

eohippus (extinct)

mastodon (extinct)

elephant

multi-
tuberculates
(extinct)

aardvark

cony

manatee

The main groups of mammals and their general relationships are shown above. The monotremes are egg-layers. Marsupials (p. 85), another primitive group, have young which are born immature. Their development continues in a marsupium, a pouch with milk glands. The placental mammals include sixteen other orders of modern mammals. Embryos of these species secure foods and oxygen and give off wastes to the mother through an intermediate structure called the placenta (p. 130).

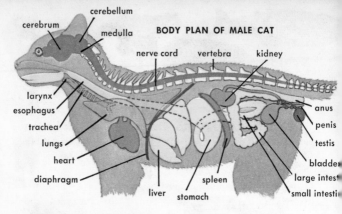

BODY PLAN OF MALE CAT

Labels: cerebrum, cerebellum, medulla, nerve cord, vertebra, kidney, larynx, esophagus, trachea, lungs, heart, diaphragm, liver, stomach, spleen, anus, penis, testis, bladder, large intestine, small intestine

BODY PLANS OF MAMMALS are basically alike. The brain center of voluntary action, thought and memory (cerebrum) is better developed than in other vertebrates. The cerebellum, important in coordination, is less prominent than in fishes and birds. The medulla controls such automatic activities as heart beat. A flat, muscular diaphragm separates chest and abdominal cavities. It assists in breathing. This is lacking or only partly developed in non-mammals.

The mammalian four-chambered heart is like that of birds, one side pumping blood to the lungs, the other pumping oxygenated blood to all parts of the body. As in other vertebrates, blood circulates in closed tubes. Arteries and veins are connected by thin-walled capillaries through which gases and liquids move to and from body cells. The liver and spleen destroy worn-out red blood cells and filter out foreign bodies from blood stream. Most male mammals have external genitals (unlike fishes, amphibians and birds which deposit sperms through a cloaca —p. 75). Major organs are pictured above.

incubating eggs   **PLATYPUS, A MONOTREME**   suckling young

EGG-LAYING MAMMALS live in Australia and a few other places. They are primitive mammals, still bearing the marks of their reptilian ancestors. These egg-laying monotremes have both the reproductive and digestive tracts opening into a cloaca through which sperms and eggs emerge. Young are hatched and raised in burrows. They lap milk from the mother's milk glands.

MARSUPIALS, or pouched mammals (kangaroo and opossum), develop young inside their bodies. While still very immature, the young crawl out of the uterus and into the marsupium, or pouch, where they attach themselves to the nipples and feed. Young opossums ride on their mothers' backs, kangaroos in the pouch. All young marsupials may crawl back into their mothers' pouches to escape danger. Marsupials are found chiefly in South America and Australia. The opossum is the only marsupial native to the U.S.

newborn opossums attached to marsupial teats

kangaroo with young in pouch   85

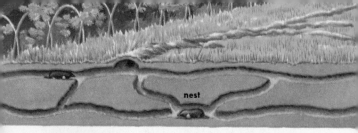

nest

mole tunnels and nest

common mole

water shrew

common brown bat

MOLES AND SHREWS are insectivores. More than half their food is insects and worms. Moles are blind or nearly so. With their broad, spadelike feet they dig tunnels just under the surface, pushing earth up into a ridge. Surface tunnels are cleared by shoving earth out as "molehills." Deeper tunnels and nests go down two feet or so.

Shrews are the smallest and fiercest of mammals. Most live in woods where debris provides protection and harbors insects. Active shrews eat several times their weight every day.

BATS have a thin, leathery membrane stretched between four long fingerbones of the forelimbs, the hind legs, and sometimes the tail. They fly at night, catching insects on the wing (vampire bats of South America feed on blood; some other bats feed on fruit). Bats have poor eyesight but easily locate or avoid objects by "radar" (or rather "sonar"), emitting a supersonic cry which echoes to their sensitive ears.

giant anteater

ANTEATERS, SLOTHS and ARMADILLOS are nearly toothless—they have only molars, and these are without enamel. Anteaters are found in the forests of tropical America. Their long front claws rip open ant and termite hills. The sticky, slender tongue which extends as much as 20 inches is flicked in and out to catch ants. Sloths hang upside-down by two or three large, hooklike claws as they travel through trees eating leaves and fruit. The single young hangs from its mother's back. Armadillos are found in southern U.S. and more widely in Central and South America. The skin of the young is leathery but adults are covered with horny plates that have movable joints. Food is mainly insects and other arthropods. Armadillos tear open ant nests with their claws, catching insects with their long, sticky tongues. They are active mainly at night.

three-toed sloth

armadillo

flying squirrel

self-sharpening rodent incisors

chipmunk

pocket gopher

THE GNAWERS—rats, squirrels and their relatives—have a pair of large chisel-like front teeth in both upper and lower jaws; the front surfaces of these are heavily enameled. Upper and lower teeth rub past each other in gnawing. This sharpens the enamel edge. Rodents are a numerous and widespread group, ranging from mice weighing only a fraction of an ounce, to 80-lb. capybaras. Porcupines, pocket gophers, guinea pigs, muskrats and beavers are rodents. More than 1600 kinds are found in North America. Rodents feed mainly on seeds, fruit and other plant material. A few are carriers of disease. Most forms serve as food for birds of prey and carnivores.

beaver house

tiger skull

CARNIVORES are predatory flesh eaters, with jaws and teeth modified for tearing and crushing. The canine teeth (lacking in rodents) are enlarged; the molars have sharp cusps. This group of quick, intelligent animals includes cats, dogs, raccoons, bears, skunks and otters. One group of carnivores has returned to the sea: walruses and seals have streamlined bodies and legs modified into flippers. Most carnivores give their young excellent care, and teach them to hunt. Since carnivores feed on flesh, they serve to control the populations of rodents and herbivores. For example, there is a clear relationship between the population cycles of hares and those of the lynx.

grizzly bear

walrus

red fox, with young in den

89

Killer whales (15 to 20 ft.)—
ferocious toothed whales

MAMMALS OF THE SEA include whales, dolphins, porpoises and the manatee (sea cow), in addition to the marine carnivores (p. 89). The baleen or toothless whales are the giants of the animal world. Despite their vast size (110 tons or more), their food consists of tiny marine crustaceans (p. 47). Baleen whales swim open-mouthed, then close their mouths, trapping food and forcing water out through sievelike whalebone. Toothed whales include dolphins, porpoises, sperm whales and the ferocious killer whale which hunts in packs. Fishes and squids are their chief foods. Sperm whales may carry a ton of sperm oil—a lubricant for precision instruments—in reservoirs in their heads.

Whales and their relatives are descendants of land mammals which returned to the sea. Their nostrils have been modified into "blow holes" at the top of their heads. Expulsion of warm, moist air forms visible spray. Whales can stay under water for an hour and have been known to dive 3600 ft. down.

Humpback whale,
length 40-50 feet

HOOFED MAMMALS — cows, horses, and their relatives are adapted to a plant diet. Their long jaws have flat-topped, ridged teeth for grinding. Many have no upper incisors, food being cropped between lower

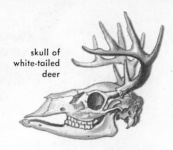

skull of white-tailed deer

teeth and hard upper gum. Animals of one group, the ruminants (sheep, cows, camels, deer, goats and antelopes), are relatively defenseless. Food is cropped rapidly and swallowed hastily. It goes into the first section of the stomach, the rumen, where it is stored (see below). The animal then moves to a safe place to "ruminate." This consists of regurgitating small masses or cuds of food which are re-chewed, then swallowed again, going into the second section, the reticulum. Water is absorbed in the third section, the omasum, and digestion gets under way in the fourth part (true stomach) and in the long intestine. Herbivores are classified into two main groups, the odd-toed species such as the horse and rhinoceros, and the even-toed such as the cow and pig.

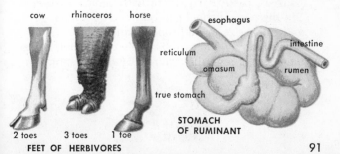

cow   rhinoceros   horse

esophagus

reticulum

intestine

omasum

rumen

true stomach

STOMACH OF RUMINANT

2 toes   3 toes   1 toe

FEET OF HERBIVORES

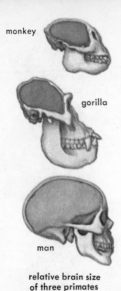

monkey

gorilla

man

relative brain size
of three primates

PRIMATES—monkeys, apes and man himself—have flattened or cupped nails on elongated fingers and toes. Opposing thumbs (see below), and opposing great toes in many species, enable primates to grasp objects. Skulls are large and brains well-developed. Front position of eyes in all except lemurs provides two separate overlapping visual images, resulting in three-dimensional vision. As shown in the family tree, primates probably descended from arboreal insectivores. Primitive primates — lemurs, tarsioids and most monkeys — live in trees.

THE GREAT APES such as the chimpanzees, orangutans and gorillas spend most of their time on the ground, retreating to trees only to sleep or avoid danger. These anthropoids (manlike primates) have larger and better developed cerebrums than the lower primates. Intelligence is high and the chimpanzees, particularly, learn with comparative ease. But there is a distinct gap between both intelligence and brain size of anthropoids and of man (above). Man's brain averages 1500 cubic centimeters; maximum size of a gorilla brain is 650 cubic centimeters.

monkey

gorilla

man

FAMILY TREE OF PRIMATES

Homo sapiens

gorilla

spider monkey

MAN

APES

NEW WORLD MONKEYS

OLD WORLD MONKEYS

marmoset

baboon

lemur

tarsier

insectivore ancestor of the primates

93

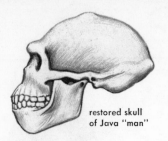

restored skull
of Java "man"

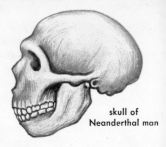

skull of
Neanderthal man

PREHISTORIC MAN has left his long record in fossil remains, tools and weapons. The most primitive remains include skulls and leg bones of Java "man" and skeletons of Peking "man." Both had ape-like characteristics—receding chins, low foreheads and heavy brow ridges. But their brain capacity was distinctly higher than that of modern apes. Their teeth were manlike, and limb bones indicate a semierect posture for Java "man" and more erect posture for Peking "man." These fossils date back some 500,000 years. Fossils of various other subhuman species have been found. Of these, Neanderthal man was the most recent. He lived in Europe and Central Asia from about 60,000 to 30,000 years ago. Skeletons show that Neanderthal man walked with a pronounced stoop. His skull was low in front, but had about the same brain volume as modern man. He was followed by Cro-Magnon man.

Neanderthal man   modern man

MODERN MAN — Homo sapiens—was first represented by the Cro-Magnons. The Neanderthals were quickly replaced by Cro-Magnons, who roamed over a wide area of Europe from about 40,000 to 15,000 years ago. Compare the pictures at the right which show how Cro-Magnon Man might have looked as compared to Neanderthal Man. These are reconstructions based on skeletons and skulls (nearly 100 Neanderthal and over 100 Cro-Magnon skeletons have been found).

Neanderthal man

Cro-Magnon was tall and erect, with the double curvature of the spine (necessary for erect posture) that is typical of modern man. Cro-Magnons had high foreheads and well-defined chins. The brain was as large as that of modern man. Cro-Magnons made tools, beads and other objects from stone, bone and shells. Beautiful paintings and carvings have been found in caves inhabited by these "Old Stone Age" men. Modern European races may be descendants of the Cro-Magnon.

Cro-Magnon man

Caucasoid

Mongoloid

Negroid

HUMAN RACES are subspecies or varieties of the species Homo sapiens. Division of modern man into distinct races is exceedingly difficult because of overlapping of the characteristics used to separate one race from another. Most commonly, Negroid, Mongoloid and Caucasoid races are recognized. Sometimes a fourth group, the Australoid, is used. Except for the primitive Australoids, all races are remarkably similar, having but superficial differences such as skin color, form of hair and shape of head. Even these characteristics do not clearly follow racial lines. For example, East Indian Caucasoids have dark skins.

All races can interbreed—proof that they belong to the same species. Modern races may have taken tens of thousands of years to develop. The pattern of their development and differentiation is not fully known. Small bands of primitive man, living for many generations in isolated regions, could develop special characteristics as a result of mutations or sudden changes in the heredity-bearing genes (p. 139).

Australoid

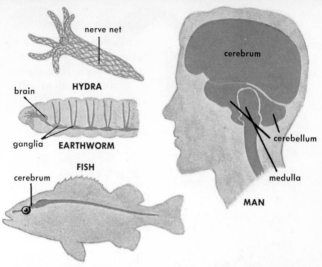

nerve net

HYDRA

brain

ganglia EARTHWORM

FISH

cerebrum

cerebrum

cerebellum

medulla

MAN

The Animal Body—How It Works

The vast diversity of animal life becomes almost incredible when one examines internal structures. All animals carry on the same basic life processes (pp. 19-21). These are handled with apparent simplicity by single-celled animals in direct contact with their environments. Higher animals have developed structures of great complexity.

The evolution of the vertebrate nervous system, which has its roots in hydra's simple network of nerve cells, culminates in the brain of man. The cerebrum—where thought, memory and other intellectual processes are centered—predominates in the human brain, but is small in fish and lacking in invertebrates. Hydra has no brain at all, yet is well adapted to its way of life.

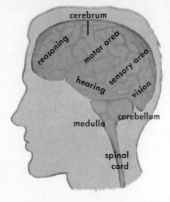

cerebrum

reasoning
motor area
sensory area
hearing
vision
cerebellum
medulla
spinal cord

NERVOUS SYSTEM of vertebrates consists of a brain, spinal cord, nerves and a specialized chain of ganglia called the autonomic system (p. 101). The brain has three main parts:

1. The brain stem or medulla is an extension of the spinal cord responsible for unconscious and involuntary control of important reflex actions, such as heart rate and breathing. The medulla also relays nerve impulses on to other parts of the brain.

2. The cerebellum is the center of coordination and balance.

3. The cerebrum is the center of voluntary actions, consciousness, and sensation. A frog, deprived of its cerebrum, wipes, furiously and accurately, to rub off acid placed on its body. So directional and coordinated action does not imply consciousness. Man's cerebrum is 85% of the brain's total weight. Cortex (outer-layer where thought and conscious activities are initiated) is folded so that its total area is about that of the body's skin.

Frog without cerebrum swims normally

NERVES are not required —nor do they exist—in one-celled animals. But animals with millions of cells must have some means of communication between cells and coordination of their activities. This is the function of nervous systems (aided by chemical regulators, p. 106). In higher animals,

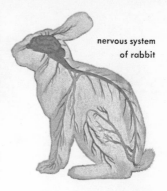
nervous system of rabbit

sensory nerves connect sense organs to the brain. Association nerves in the spinal cord and brain act like switchboards, carrying sensory messages to motor nerves which stimulate muscles or glands to act. Thought takes place in the millions of association nerves of the cerebral cortex.

THE "REFLEX ARC," simplest example of the action of sensory and motor nerves, is shown below. A pin prick on the hand stimulates a sensory message which travels up a nerve to the spinal cord. The impulse travels back through a motor nerve to muscles which jerk the hand back involuntarily. A fraction of a second later the sensory impulse reaches the brain, where pain is felt and where decisions on what to do next are made and relayed down the cord.

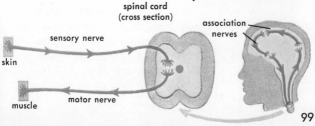
spinal cord
(cross section)

association nerves

sensory nerve

skin

motor nerve

muscle

normal curiosity

conditioned fear

CONDITIONED REFLEXES are modified reflex arcs. The physiologist, Pavlov, found that if food is placed before a hungry dog, saliva will flow in its mouth. The sight and smell of food trigger a reflex arc, starting the secretion. Pavlov rang a bell every time food was given to a dog. After many repetitions, the sound of the bell produced salivary secretions even when no food was offered. The original reflex—*smell of food→flow of saliva*—had been conditioned or modified to another arc: *sound of bell→flow of saliva*.

Many human acts and reactions (see above) are results of conditioning which, however, involves cerebral association centers.

PERCEPTION, insight and purpose, not reflex arcs, determine our reactions to most things. Do you perceive the picture at the left as a vase or as two heads?

AUTONOMIC NERVOUS SYSTEM in the higher vertebrates normally operates beyond voluntary control. It automatically affects such functions as secretion of digestive juices, constriction of blood vessels and action of heart. The autonomic system consists of a chain of ganglia or miniature "switchboards" and nerves. In form and function it is comparable to the entire nervous system of the earthworm and other lower animals. Some of these ganglia are located in the medulla and spinal cord.

The operation involves reflex arcs between sensory nerves and motor nerves. The nervous systems of some lower animals permit only instinctive, unlearned, reflex-type activities. The autonomic system in higher vertebrates provides a similar automatic control of vital body processes. It partly frees the central nervous system for control and coordination of voluntary activity. But each ganglion of the autonomic system is connected to a nerve of the spinal cord, providing a route for nerve impulses between the central and the autonomic systems. Thus the rate of the heart's beat, basically beyond voluntary control, may be increased or decreased by thoughts originating in the cerebrum.

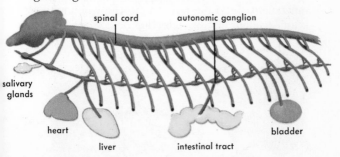

RELATION OF CENTRAL AND AUTONOMIC NERVOUS SYSTEMS 101

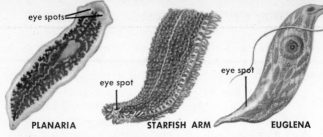

eye spots

PLANARIA

eye spot

STARFISH ARM

eye spot

EUGLENA

SENSE ORGANS show a gradual increase in complexity from lower to higher animals. The protoplasm of protozoa is sensitive to light, touch, heat and chemicals. But some protozoa such as Euglena and planaria (a flatworm), starfish and jellyfish, all have light-sensitive pigment spots. Higher animals have specialized structures for sight, hearing, smell, taste, touch and pain.

LIGHT RECEPTORS vary from light-sensitive spots in lower forms to the complex image-forming eyes of birds and mammals. Simple eyes of spiders, insects and snails have fixed lenses and cannot focus. Each section of the compound eyes of insects and other arthropods (below) is a separate light receptor. Insects see a mosaic of light and shadow. The slightest movement shifts the pattern. So the compound eye is an excellent motion-detecting device.

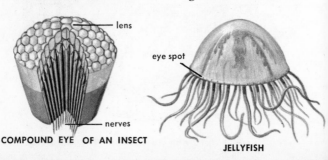

lens

nerves

COMPOUND EYE OF AN INSECT

eye spot

JELLYFISH

THE EYES of squids and octopuses are remarkably like eyes of vertebrates—they form clear, focused images. The human eye, shown below, is typical of vertebrate eyes. Light enters through the transparent cornea, is focused by the elastic lens, and forms an inverted image on the retina, which the brain interprets as upright. The opaque iris is an automatic diaphragm, constantly adjusting the size of the lens opening, or pupil, according to the amount of light available. The lens automatically thickens or thins to bend light from near and far objects to focus on the retina. The retina has two kinds of specialized nerve endings: rods, adapted for colorless vision in dim light, and cones which function in bright light and are sensitive to both white and colored light.

CROSS SECTION OF HUMAN EYE

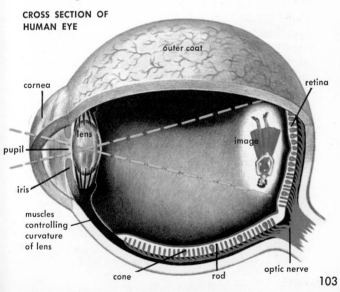

outer coat

cornea

retina

lens

image

pupil

iris

muscles controlling curvature of lens

cone

rod

optic nerve

KATYDID   **TURKEY VULTURE**

HEARING is the perception of a series of vibrations or compression waves in air or water. Humans hear, as sound, such waves which vibrate from about 20 to 16,000 times per second. Bats, dogs, some insects and other animals hear sounds beyond the range of human hearing. Earthworms detect vibrations in the ground, such as those produced by walking. Other lower animals also respond to slow, but intense vibrations, though they cannot hear.

In the ear a membrane, which sound waves cause to vibrate, transmits vibrations to nerve endings. Position and form of ears vary greatly. Katydid "ears" are on its front legs. Grasshoppers' are on the abdomen. Birds have outer ear canals but no external flaps. Fish have neither outer ears nor eardrums. Sound is communicated through head bones to nerves of the inner ear. The fish's lateral line detects slow vibrations reflected from nearby objects.

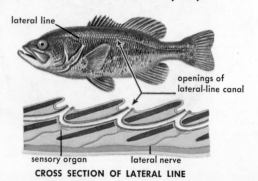

CROSS SECTION OF LATERAL LINE

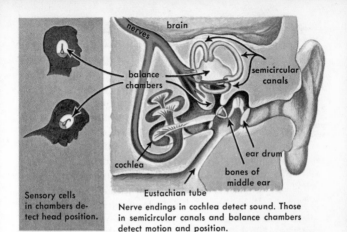

Nerve endings in cochlea detect sound. Those in semicircular canals and balance chambers detect motion and position.

Sensory cells in chambers detect head position.

VERTEBRATE EARS are usually like the human ears shown above. Vibrations in air are carried by the eardrum, to bones of middle ear, hence to a fluid-filled cochlea. Vibrations in this fluid stimulate ciliated "hair" cells attached to nerve endings. Different nerve endings are "tuned" to different frequencies somewhat like the strings of a piano.

SENSE OF BALANCE is assisted by two kinds of balance organs in inner ear. 1. Three fluid-filled semicircular canals, each in a different plane, detect head movements. Motion causes the fluid to move, stimulating nerve endings. 2. Two tiny chambers are lined with hairlike nerves, each with a limey end. Gravity bends hairs, indicating the head's position. Crayfish fills statocyst with grains of sand, which indicate body position by pressing against nerve endings.

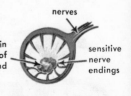

STATOCYST OF CRAYFISH

105

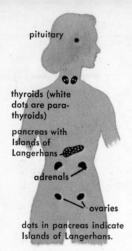

pituitary

thyroids (white
dots are para-
thyroids)

pancreas with
Islands of
Langerhans

adrenals

ovaries

dots in pancreas indicate
Islands of Langerhans.

CHEMICAL REGULATORS—hormones—help coordinate body functions. The endocrine glands which produce them have no ducts. Secretions flow directly into blood. Thus every cell in the body is potentially affected. Metamorphosis of insects (p. 56) is probably due to hormonal activity. Hormones also probably account for metamorphosis of amphibia. For example, the salamander, Ambystoma (see below) normally changes from a gill-breathing larva into a lung-breathing adult. In some regions the adult retains its gills and has no lungs—probably as a result of thyroid deficiency. Such an adult is called Axolotl and was formerly considered a separate species. When fed thyroid extract, Axolotl changes into Ambystoma.

The diagram above locates the endocrine glands in the human body. The pituitary lies at the base of the brain; thyroids lie saddle-like over the voice box; parathyroids are embedded in thyroids; islands of Langerhans are scattered in the pancreas, a digestive gland; adrenals are on top of the kidneys.

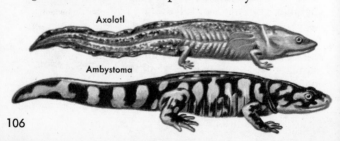

Axolotl

Ambystoma

Pituitary, the "master gland," produces a group of hormones regulating other endocrine glands. One hormone controls growth, an excess causing giantism and a coarsening of features. A deficiency causes dwarfism.

Thyroid affects oxidation of food in cells, regulating metabolism. One milligram (a speck) will increase metabolism of 150 lb. man 2% for day.

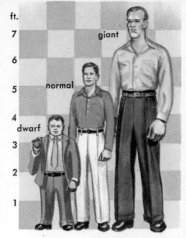

Parathyroids control the calcium level in blood. Severe calcium deficiency in animals causes convulsion and death in a few days.

Islands of Langerhans secrete insulin, controlling sugar metabolism. Inadequate secretion causes diabetes. This disease may be controlled by insulin.

Adrenal glands secrete adrenalin much faster than usual during fright or anger. This increases the heart rate, dilates lung tubes, raises blood pressure. Adrenal cortex or outside layer secretes a hormone controlling level of salts in the blood.

Sex glands—testes in male; ovaries in female—produce hormones as well as sex cells. These hormones control secondary sex characteristics like the beard in man, breasts in woman and ovulation (egg-production) cycle (p. 129), including menstruation.

Female chick develops male traits from injection of male hormones.

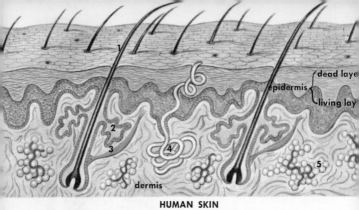

HUMAN SKIN

1. hair shaft	4. sweat gland
2. oil gland	5. stored fat
3. erector muscle	

SKIN AND ITS DERIVATIVES Every organism has some kind of membrane or skin. Such coverings protect the soft living protoplasm against injury, the invasion of disease organisms, and against drying out.

Vertebrate bodies are encased in a tough, elastic skin which is continuous with a membrane that completely lines the digestive tube and other body openings. Hence, when food is swallowed, it is still outside the body proper. Digestion changes food into a form that can go through the membrane of the intestinal wall and enter the body itself.

Human skin is extremely complicated. It is composed of two layers: an outer epidermis and an inner dermis. The living, inner part of the epidermis is made of rapidly dividing cells. As the cells push outward, they die, forming a tough protective skin layer. Skin contains oil and sweat glands, blood vessels and nerves.

Dead epidermal cells slough off continuously. Usually unnoticed except when sunburn causes patches of epidermis to peel off, ordinary shedding is part of the normal growing process. The scalp has more oil glands. Their secretion sticks dead cells together into larger plaques—dandruff.

reptilian scales

SKIN DERIVATIVES include nails, claws, antlers, hooves, scales, hair and feathers. All these grow from specialized skin cells. Even tooth enamel is a development from these cells. All these skin derivatives have a similar origin. Hair and feathers are shed periodically or gradually.

Hair and feathers protect against physical injury and against heat loss. Tiny muscles attached to the bases of hairs and feathers are controlled by the autonomic system (p. 101). When contracted, these muscles cause the hairs or feathers to stand erect. This provides an excellent insulation in cold weather. It is also a fright or anger reaction in some animals. "Goose pimples" in human beings (in cold weather or fright) are produced by these tiny muscles when they contract in our skin.

fish scales

feather

tooth

claws

nail

EPIDERMAL
STRUCTURES

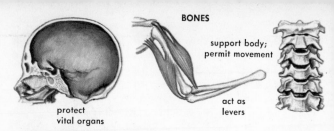

BONES

support body;
permit movement

protect
vital organs

act as
levers

BONES AND SKELETONS provide the framework and support of vertebrate bodies. Bone is a living tissue, the cells of which form deposits of calcium salts. Held together by ligaments, bones act as levers on which muscles can act. The humerus (upper arm bone), for example, anchors and acts as a lever for muscles. Other bones, such as skull and ribs, protect vital body parts.

The spinal column is composed of saddle-like vertebrae tightly laced together with strong ligaments; yet it is flexible. A large, lengthwise hole in each vertebra provides a protected passageway for the spinal cord. Paired openings between vertebrae permit spinal nerves to leave the cord. Vertebrae are separated by cartilage pads (not shown in picture) which act as shock absorbers.

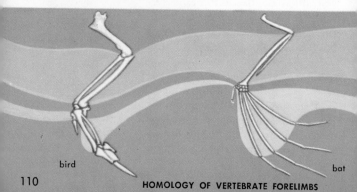

bird

bat

HOMOLOGY OF VERTEBRATE FORELIMBS

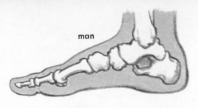

FOOT POSITIONS IN WALKING

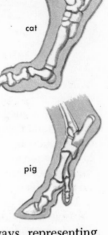

HOMOLOGOUS STRUCTURES

(same, but differently adapted parts) of mammalian feet are shown at the right. A comparison of vertebrate forearms is shown below. The skeletons of mammals are very much alike—almost bone for bone—in the basic parts. But the individual bones have evolved in different ways, representing adaptations to different environments. Note particularly the different shapes and positions of the heel and toe bones in human, cat and pig feet. Man walks on his whole foot, the cat on its toes, and the pig on its enlarged toenails, or hooves.

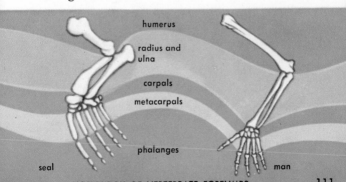

HOMOLOGY OF VERTEBRATE FORELIMBS

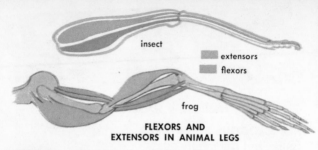

**FLEXORS AND
EXTENSORS IN ANIMAL LEGS**

MUSCLES produce movement by their ability to contract. Skeletal muscles are arranged in pairs or layers. *Flexors,* such as the biceps which draws the forearm up, are matched with *extensors,* such as the triceps which straightens out the forearm. Coordination of many muscles enables human hands to perform such intricate actions as playing the piano or typing.

Muscle fibers are attached to bones by tough tendons. Ligaments (tough, white, flexible bands) usually attach bones firmly together at the joints, but they also hold muscles and other organs in place. About 500 muscles are found in the human body.

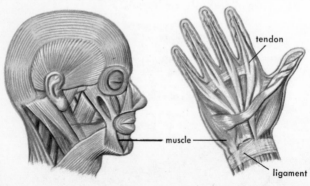

MUSCLES AND TENDONS

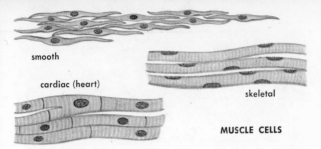

smooth

cardiac (heart)

skeletal

MUSCLE CELLS

THREE KINDS OF MUSCLE CELLS are found in verte-brates. Smooth muscles, controlled by the autonomic nervous system (p. 101) produce involuntary move-ments—as of the iris of the eye. Cardiac or heart muscle cells are found only in vertebrate hearts. These cells are closely interconnected, and a single nerve impulse causes an entire group to contract at once. Skeletal or voluntary muscles respond quickly. Each cell responds to nerve stimulation by a com-plete contraction. Small movements of the arm repre-sent full contraction of relatively few cells. Further movement results from contraction of more cells.

CILIATED CELLS provide movement for many proto-zoa and other small animals (p. 26); vertebrates use them for special purposes. The windpipe and its small branches in the lungs are lined with them. Inhaled dust is whipped to the back of throat by wavelike motion of the cilia.

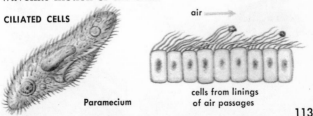

CILIATED CELLS

air →

Paramecium

cells from linings
of air passages

Predators have powerful jaws, sharp teeth and claws

Archer fish squirts water to dislodge insect.

SECURING AND USING FOOD is a primary necessity of animal existence. Food provides energy and materials for maintaining and repairing living protoplasm. Eating, digestion, assimilation of food and removal of wastes are all involved in food utilization. Earlier pages (pp. 19-20) have shown how lower animals get and use food. Pictured here are some vertebrate food-getting adaptations. The following pages show structural adaptations for the use of foods.

Rattlesnake fangs inject poison.

Chameleon catches insects with sticky tongue.

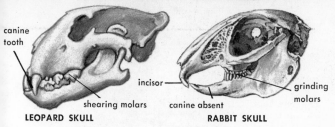

canine tooth

incisor

grinding molars

shearing molars

canine absent

LEOPARD SKULL

RABBIT SKULL

MEAT EATERS AND PLANT EATERS show both external and internal adaptations which equip them to handle the food they eat. The large canine teeth and shearing molars of carnivorous mammals are matched by an intestinal tract equipped for effective handling of meat.

Herbivorous animals usually have large cropping or cutting incisors, and large, ridged, grinding molars. Their intestines are relatively long to permit the necessarily slow digestion of plant fibers. The caecum, an important part of the digestive tract of many herbivorous animals, is almost absent in carnivores.

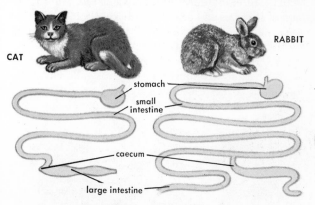

RABBIT

CAT

stomach

small intestine

caecum

large intestine

DIGESTIVE TRACTS OF CAT AND RABBIT DRAWN TO SAME SCALE

115

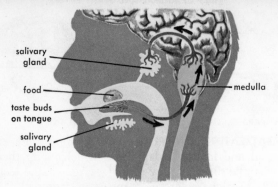

Flow of saliva is stimulated by sense of taste.

DIGESTION changes complex food molecules into simple ones that can be absorbed and used by living cells. In higher animals such changes are also necessary so that foods can pass through the intestinal wall into the blood stream. Starch, for example, is a large molecule that cannot pass through intestinal walls. Digestion breaks it down into small sugar molecules which are easily absorbed. Saliva begins the digestion of starches and other carbohydrates in some animals. Salivary glands are activated by sense of taste, by odors, or even the thought of food (all reflexes— see p. 99). Nerve paths from taste buds to the parotid salivary gland are shown above. In swallowing, the epiglottis covers the opening to the windpipe (trachea) so that no food will enter, as shown below.

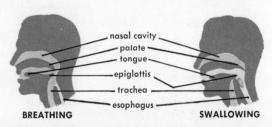

BREATHING   SWALLOWING

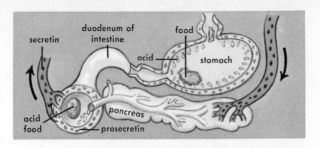

The stomach, chiefly a storage organ, begins protein digestion. Vigorous movements of the stomach mix food and juices, changing food to a semi-liquid. Most digestion takes place in the small intestines. Carbohydrate and protein digestion is completed and fats are fully digested here. Intestinal glands, the pancreas and the liver aid in digesting by secreting juices into the intestines. A chemical action—not nerves—causes the pancreas to secrete (see picture above). Prosecretin in intestinal wall changes to secretin when acid food goes by. This flows through blood stream to pancreas, causing it to secrete.

Digested food is absorbed through minute finger-like projections (villi) of the small intestine (below). Fats pass into lacteals, carbohydrates and proteins into capillaries.

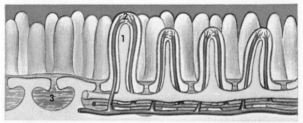

Villi of intestine, showing lacteals (1), capillary (2) and glands (3).

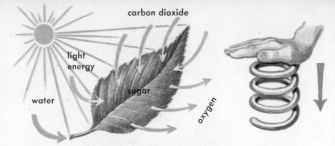

Photosynthesis occurs only in plants. It is the chemical equivalent of depressing a spring: energy is stored.

ENERGY is released as foods are "burned" in body cells. The energy of foods comes originally from sunlight. Green plants combine carbon dioxide with water to produce sugars and oxygen. Light is required for this process of photosynthesis which converts solar energy into the chemical energy of sugar. Cellular respiration chemically combines food and oxygen, releasing energy. Chemically, respiration is the reverse of photosynthesis. Water and carbon dioxide are given off as wastes when sugar is "burned" in animal cells. Materials in protein and fats are also "burned," with release of energy and wastes.

Respiration occurs in both plants and animals. It is the equivalent of releasing a spring: energy is released.

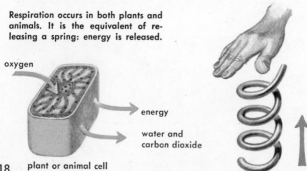

plant or animal cell

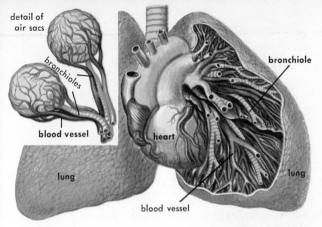

detail of air sacs

bronchioles

blood vessel

lung

bronchiole

heart

blood vessel

lung

OXYGEN must be provided continuously to living cells. Very simple animals are in direct contact with air or oxygen dissolved in water. But higher animals require complex breathing systems (above). Lungs of mammals consist of branching air tubes (bronchioles) ending in air sacs surrounded by networks of capillaries. Oxygen and carbon dioxide are exchanged through membranes of sacs and capillaries. Inhaling results from expansion of chest cavity, as shown below. Outside air pressure forces air into lungs, as there is less pressure between lungs and chest wall. Decreasing chest cavity reverses the process.

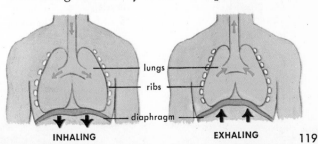

lungs

ribs

diaphragm

INHALING   **EXHALING**

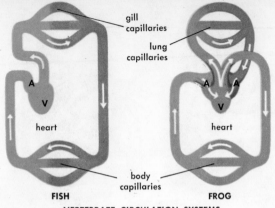

gill capillaries

lung capillaries

A

V

heart

A A

V

heart

body capillaries

FISH

FROG

VERTEBRATE CIRCULATION SYSTEMS

A = auricle
V = ventricle
▬ = blood rich in oxygen
▬ = blood poor in oxygen

CIRCULATORY SYSTEMS vary greatly. Insects have but one blood vessel—a pulsating "heart" tube with an opening at the head end and paired openings in the sides at the abdominal region. Pulsations draw blood through side openings and out the head opening. The "open circulation" causes a slow flow of blood which bathes tissues of the insect's body. Earthworms, vertebrates and some other groups have "closed circulation" systems. In these, blood is confined in arteries, capillaries and veins. Liquid

"heart" tube

OPEN CIRCULATION OF INSECT

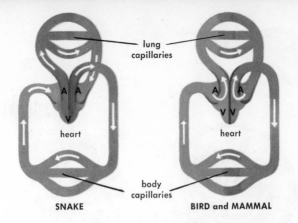

lung capillaries

A A
V
heart

A A
V V
heart

body capillaries

SNAKE

BIRD and MAMMAL

portions of the blood and substances in solution (food, oxygen, hormones) pass through capillary walls into the cells.

Vertebrates' systems are much alike. But the two-chambered heart of fishes must force blood through gill capillaries, then directly to body cells under reduced pressure. Amphibians have three-chambered hearts. Oxygen-rich blood from the lungs and oxygen-poor blood from the body cells are mixed in the single ventricle. A partial separation between halves of single ventricle in the snake heart permits the same kind of mixing on a smaller scale. Four chambers of mammalian and bird hearts permit only oxygen-rich blood to be pumped to the body cells.

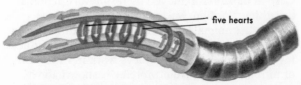

five hearts

CLOSED CIRCULATION OF EARTHWORM

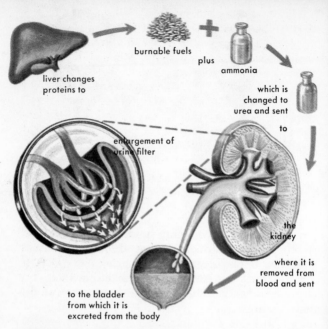

liver changes proteins to

burnable fuels

plus

ammonia

which is changed to urea and sent

to

enlargement of urine filter

the kidney

where it is removed from blood and sent

to the bladder from which it is excreted from the body

WASTE REMOVAL is essential to all animal life. Undigested materials in the digestive tract are not true body wastes for they have never entered the body proper. The entire digestive tract is lined with a membrane. Only digested materials can pass. But cellular activities produce chemical wastes which must be removed from the body via the blood stream. Carbon dioxide is removed by respiratory action and breathing. Protein wastes are toxic to animal cells and higher animals have different structures such as green glands (p. 46), tubules (p. 55) and kidneys for their removal. How kidneys work in the removal of nitrogen wastes from proteins is shown above.

SWEAT GLANDS AND THERMOSTATS. Temperature of warm-blooded animals remains practically constant. Heat control is automatic. Much of the work in many animals is done by sweat glands. Water in sweat evaporates, absorbing heat from skin, and cooling the blood in the skin. Secretion of sweat varies automatically with body's cooling needs, increasing rapidly in hot weather or during physical activity. Dogs and some other animals lack sweat glands. Their bodies are cooled partly by copious salivary secretion which evaporates rapidly during panting and partly by exhalation of warm air.

Expansion of surface blood vessels (flushed skin) in hot weather results from stimulation of heat-sensitive nerves. More blood is brought to surface and more heat is lost by radiation. Cold-sensitive nerves contract surface blood vessels, shifting blood deeper inside the body. "Goose-pimples" in humans are caused by contraction of erectile hair muscles in the skin (p. 109).

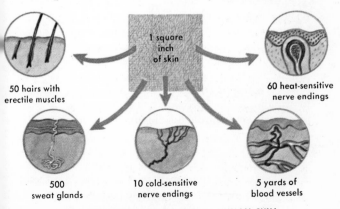

1 square inch of skin

50 hairs with erectile muscles

60 heat-sensitive nerve endings

500 sweat glands

10 cold-sensitive nerve endings

5 yards of blood vessels

HEAT-REGULATING STRUCTURES IN HUMAN SKIN

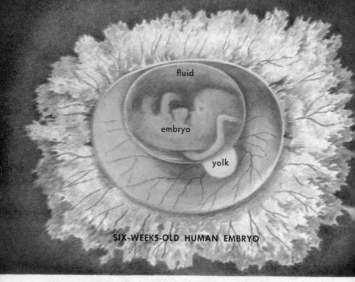

SIX-WEEKS-OLD HUMAN EMBRYO

fluid

embryo

yolk

Maintaining the Race

REPRODUCTION involves far more than just the division of cells as in asexual reproduction (p. 126) or the simple union of cells as in sexual reproduction. Each of these apparently simple processes involves a precise duplication of inheritance factors or genes (p. 133). Reproduction, inheritance, and the development of embryos (unborn or unhatched young) all help maintain the race.

An early stage in the development of a human embryo is pictured above. Floating in a watery fluid, the embryo is nourished and protected by the mother's body, its wastes being removed through a placenta (p. 130). Other ways of feeding and protecting embryos and young are shown on next page.

SCORPION, a relative of the spiders, bears its young alive from eggs hatched within the body. The baby scorpions cling to the mother's body with their pincerlike mouth parts.

SEA CATFISH males, and males of some African fresh-water fishes, carry eggs in their mouths until hatched. Baby fish use male's mouth as home—occasionally darting out.

COWBIRD female lays eggs in another bird's nest. Eggs hatch in ten days—sooner than those of most other birds. The cowbirds then secure the most food from the foster mother.

GIANT WATER BUG female cements eggs to back of male. Eggs are protected by this attachment to large, voracious adult.

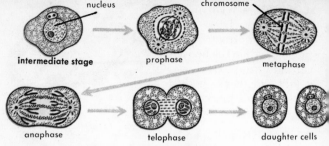

ASEXUAL REPRODUCTION BY MITOSIS

REPRODUCTION WITHOUT SEX usually occurs in single-celled animals by division (fission). Basic to fission is the mechanism by which the nuclear contents of the cell arrange themselves and divide. Strands of nuclear material called chromosomes go through various phases as shown above. Each chromosome duplicates lengthwise into identical pairs. In the metaphase, the paired chromosomes line up at the equator of the nucleus. The pairs separate and one member of each pair goes to each daughter cell. The result is that both daughter cells receive the same inheritance factors.

ASEXUAL REPRODUCTION BY FISSION AND BUDDING

fission of trypanosome

dividing of anemone by budding

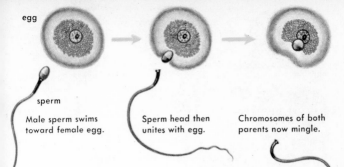

egg

sperm

Male sperm swims toward female egg.

Sperm head then unites with egg.

Chromosomes of both parents now mingle.

SEXUAL REPRODUCTION results when two sex cells unite. In higher animals the male sex cell or sperm swims to and enters the larger female sex cell or egg. The sperm tail usually drops off as the head unites with the egg. The fertilized egg then divides by the process of mitosis pictured at the top of opposite page. Growth involves repeated division. Each division provides the daughter cells with chromosomal material from *both* the original sperm and egg cells. Thus, every organism, sexually produced, carries chromosomes from both parents. Protozoans sometimes unite sexually, as shown below.

CONJUGATION: typical process in the Paramecium.

ISOGAMY: two similar cells of Chlamydomonas unite.

HETEROGAMY: in higher animals dissimilar cells unite.

127

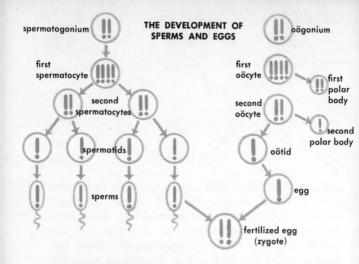

spermatogonium

THE DEVELOPMENT OF SPERMS AND EGGS

oögonium

first spermatocyte

first oöcyte

first polar body

second spermatocytes

second oöcyte

second polar body

spermatids

oötid

sperms

egg

fertilized egg (zygote)

SPERMS AND EGGS arise in testes and ovaries. Special cells (spermatogonia, oögonia) divide by mitosis to form many cells. Each new spermatogonium or oögonium has the same number and kind of chromosomes as the original fertilized egg. In the first spermatocyte and first oöcyte pairs of chromosomes duplicate, forming tetrads. In the two following divisions (meiosis) the number of chromosomes is reduced. Finally each spermatid and oötid has only half as many chromosomes as the original cell. During the development of the egg, polar bodies degenerate; the oöcyte results in one egg, the first spermatocyte in four sperms. When egg is fertilized, pairs of similar chromosomes reform; one member of each pair comes from each parent. The above diagram is simplified. Humans and tobacco plants both have 24 pairs of chromosomes.

HUMAN REPRODUCTION involves eggs, sperms and internal fertilization. Sperms are produced by the billions in the testes (see diagram at right). They move through a duct past the seminal vesicle and prostate gland. Each of these contributes a fluid in which the sperms

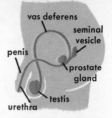

MALE REPRODUCTIVE TRACT

are carried through the urethra in the penis and into the vagina of the female. Of the millions of sperms deposited in the female, only one will unite with each egg. The rest die.

Eggs develop in the ovary in a regular monthly cycle (see diagram below). They break through the ovary wall in ovulation and fall into the funnel-like opening of the fallopian tube or oviduct. Fertilization occurs in this tube and the rapidly dividing fertilized egg embeds in the uterine wall where it is nourished and protected. If unfertilized, the egg disintegrates. Uterine lining sloughs off in the process of menstruation.

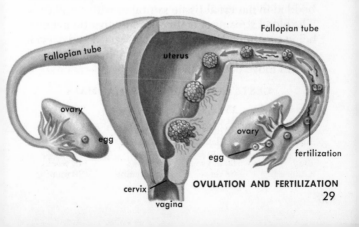

OVULATION AND FERTILIZATION

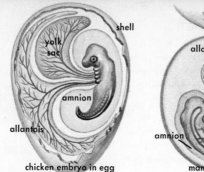

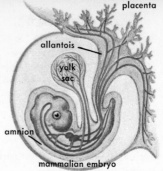

chicken embryo in egg

mammalian embryo

OVIPAROUS　　　　　　　**VIVIPAROUS**

EMBRYONIC DEVELOPMENT in egg-laying animals and in the placental mammals is much alike. Both chick and mammalian embryos float in a liquid-filled amniotic cavity. Chick embryo secures nourishment from yolk, throwing wastes into a special sac, the allantois. Respiration is through the shell.

Most mammalian embryos have a yolk sac, but little or no yolk is used, as the embryo secures food from its mother through a placenta. The placenta consists of a network of embryonic capillaries imbedded in maternal tissue saturated with capillaries. The blood streams of embryo and mother do not mix, being separated by membranes. But food and oxygen move into embryo blood stream from the mother, and wastes move out into the mother's bloodstream.

GESTATION PERIODS OF MAMMALS

Opossum	13 days	Pig	16 weeks
Mouse	21 days	Sheep	21 weeks
Rat	22 days	Monkey	24 weeks
Rabbit	32 days	Man	36 weeks
Cat	60 days	Cow	40 weeks
Dog	60 days	Horse	48 weeks
Guinea pig	68 days	Elephant	20 months

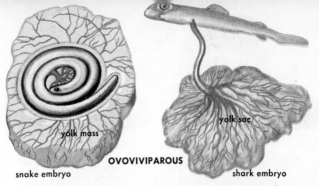

OVOVIVIPAROUS

yolk mass

snake embryo

yolk sac

shark embryo

Some non-mammalian animals also develop their embryos inside their bodies but without nourishment from the mother. Such animals are called *ovoviviparous*—young are born, but are nourished from egg yolks. Scorpions, garter snakes, rattlesnakes, as well as sharks, and several other fishes are ovoviviparous. Eggs vary greatly in size and form, and in the number laid. Frog and toad eggs are laid by the thousands and after fertilization develop a protective gelatinous covering. Fish eggs are laid by the hundreds of thousands and are then fertilized by milt (sperms) from the male. Gestation, the period of time in which mammalian young are carried in the uterus, varies considerably. So does the incubation period for eggs of birds.

INCUBATION PERIODS OF BIRD EGGS

Yellow Warbler	11 days	Great Blue	
Robin	12 days	Heron	25-28 days
Bluebird	13-16 days	Goose	28 days
Barn Swallow	14-16 days	Loon	28 days
Chimney Swift	18 days	Swan	35 days
Chicken	21 days	Ostrich	42 days
Flicker	23-26 days	Eagle	43 days
Killdeer	25 days	Albatross	56 days

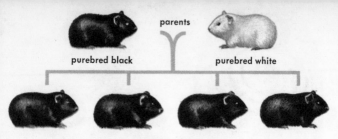

parents

purebred black   purebred white

all black offspring

INHERITANCE The appearance of an animal does not necessarily reveal its heredity. Sexual reproduction involves the union of sex cells (p. 127); hence a fertilized egg has *pairs* of chromosomes—one of each pair coming from each parent. Every cell in the animal developing from that egg bears chromosomes from both its father and its mother. These determine its inheritance; but their effects although often obvious, are also sometimes masked.

When a purebred black and a purebred white guinea pig (above) are mated, the offspring receive a chromosome bearing the factor for black coat from one parent and one bearing the factor for white coat from the other. But all appear black! The factor for white color is not effective when the factor for black is present. That it is there, none the less, is proven when two of these offspring are mated (below). Black and white young appear in the ratio of three to one.

parents

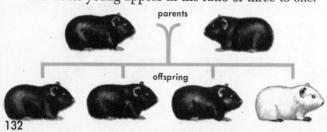

offspring

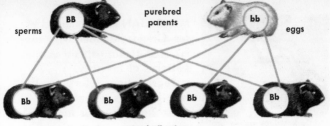

sperms — purebred parents — eggs

BB   bb

Bb   Bb   Bb   Bb

mixed offspring

GENETICS EXPLAINS INHERITANCE in terms of genes. Genes, found on every chromosome (p. 134), determine inheritance. A purebred black guinea pig has a pair of genes for black color in each body cell. These genes separate when sperms are produced. So each sperm has but one of these genes for black. The genes for white color also separate when a purebred white mother produces eggs. Offspring receive a single gene for color from each parent (above); hence all are genetically mixed for color. But the gene for white color is recessive (it is masked by the gene for black), so the offspring appear black. When these offspring are mated (chart below) their young appear in the ratio of three black to one white. One of the black is purebred, each cell having two genes for black color. Two are mixed for color, having one gene for black and one for white. One is white, having no genes for black to mask the genes for white.

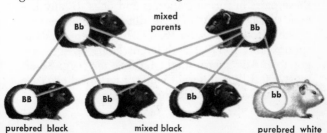

mixed parents

Bb   Bb

BB   Bb   Bb   bb

purebred black   mixed black   purebred white

James Kitzmiller

Dark strings above are mosquito chromosomes.

MENDELIAN LAWS, named after Gregor Mendel who discovered them, explain simple patterns of heredity.

Segregation refers to the fact that pairs of genes, such as those for hair color in guinea pigs, always separate so that sperms and eggs have but *one* gene of a pair—never two or one and a half.

Independent assortment refers to the fact that the genes for any particular characteristic, such as hair color, generally separate independently from those for other characteristics, such as hair texture. But independent assortment cannot occur among genes located on the same chromosome; these are linked together and ordinarily move as a unit.

Dominance, which occurs in the inheritance of many but not all traits, is the masking of a gene by another in a pair. In the guinea pig, the gene for white color is masked by the gene for black color.

POSSIBLE NUMBERS OF GENE COMBINATIONS. Even two pairs of genes result in many different combinations, as shown on the next page. There are 24 pairs of chromosomes in human beings, bearing thousands of genes. Meiosis (p. 128) separates these pairs in forming sperms and eggs. In any human this permits 16,777,216 different combinations of the chromosomes. So 16,777,216 different kinds of sperms and 16,777,216 different kinds of eggs are possible. Any sperm might fertilize any egg. So almost 300 trillion different kinds of fertilized eggs are possible. Each human is literally unique!

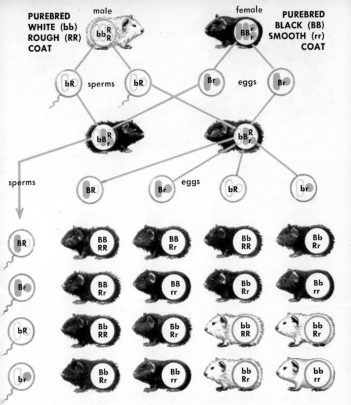

DIHYBRID (TWO-CHARACTERISTIC) CROSS produces mixed offspring as shown at top. Black (B) is dominant over white (b), and rough coat (R) is dominant over smooth coat (r). So offspring are all black with rough coats. When these are mated any of four kinds of sperms can unite with any of four kinds of eggs. Offspring are black-rough, black-smooth, white-rough, and white-smooth in a 9:3:3:1 ratio.

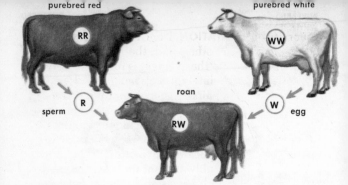

purebred red
RR

purebred white
WW

roan

sperm
R

RW

egg
W

BLENDING, or incomplete dominance, results in an intermediate mixture of contrasting traits, as in blending in colors of Shorthorn cattle. Roan color is actually a mixture of red and white hairs on coat. Red or white cattle are purebred for hair color, but all roan cattle are mixed for hair color.

MULTIPLE ALLELES result from effects of three or more alternative genes at same position on a chromosome. Blood groups in human beings are an example. Three genes, A, A^B and a all affect blood type. A and A^B are both dominant over a, but neither is dominant to the other. So when A and A^B are together, the AB blood group results. Chart shows other gene combinations. Blood grouping is used to determine whether a given male could be the father of a certain child. A child with blood type A whose mother has type B could *not* be the child of a father with O or B blood. It *might* be the child of a father with AB or A blood.

BLOOD GROUPS	GENES
A	A^a or AA
B	$A^B A^B$ or $A^B a$
AB	$A A^B$
O	a^a

CONTINUOUS VARIATION from one extreme of a characteristic to the other, with the majority of offspring found close to the average, is found for many characteristics like intelligence, height and body build. Ten or more pairs of genes (multiple factors), some on different chromosomes, are probably responsible for height. This may provide for thousands of different heights (and such environmental factors as diet further complicate the picture). Far more multiple factors probably account for inherited intelligence. Skin color in human beings results from action of two or more pairs of genes. These have a blending action, and two pairs would produce five color gradations (charted below) if mixed offspring of purebred parents mated.

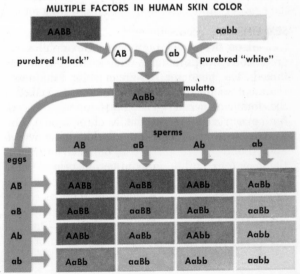

MULTIPLE FACTORS IN HUMAN SKIN COLOR

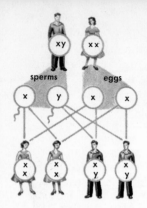

sperms   eggs

SEX of the offspring is determined by genes when the sperm unites with the egg. One pair of chromosomes are called sex chromosomes. The two are alike in females and are called X chromosomes. Males have one X chromosome and one tiny Y chromosome. When sperms and eggs are produced, the chromosomes separate. So half the sperms are X sperms and half are Y sperms, but all eggs have X chromosomes. There is equal chance of an X sperm or a Y sperm fertilizing the egg. XY produces a male; XX produces a female.

SEX LINKAGE occurs because other genes are also located on the sex chromosomes. Hemophilia, red-green color blindness, and other conditions are sex-linked. The gene for red-green color blindness is recessive, so the defect will not occur if masked by the dominant normal gene. Furthermore, the genes for color vision are on the X chromosome. So a woman with *one* gene for colorblindness will *be* normal and see red and green, but she can transmit the gene for colorblindness to her offspring.

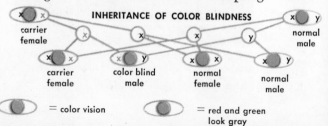

INHERITANCE OF COLOR BLINDNESS

carrier female

normal male

carrier female

color blind male

normal female

normal male

= color vision   = red and green look gray

Ancon sheep

normal sheep

MUTATIONS are changes in the genes which produce new characteristics in the offspring. Such offspring are called mutants or sports. They may breed true in regard to the new characteristics. Mutations are common but generally produce slight, unnoticeable changes. Occasionally, however, a mutation is prominent and valuable. In 1791, a male lamb with short, bent legs was born on a Massachusetts farm. Because the short legs prevented it from jumping fences, the mutant was used in breeding to establish the famous Ancon breed of sheep.

Many gene mutations are recessive. Because the recessive mutant characteristic is marked by that of the dominant gene with which it pairs (p. 133), it only appears later when two of the recessive mutant genes chance to be paired. This could occur only from mating descendants of the original mutant.

horned
Hereford

polled
Hereford

Manx
cat

silver fox

SURVIVAL VALUE OF MUTATIONS is usually limited. Laboratory research indicates that many mutations are harmful to the species, making the mutant less likely to survive and produce offspring than its fellows. Normal Hereford cattle, for example, have horns. But a mutant variety, the polled Hereford, is hornless. This makes the animals safer to handle, but the same mutation in wild animals would decrease their defenses. Experimental mutations produced by radiation of fruit flies are often harmful. Note stunted wings and eyeless form below. Most mutations (the short-tailed Manx cat, the silver fox) probably have little effect on survival. The occurrence of mutations with positive survival value may account for evolutionary change (p. 142).

MUTATIONS IN FRUIT FLY

normal
wing

vestigial
wing

club
wing

normal
eye

eyeless

barred
eye

ADAPTATIONS AND SURVIVAL. A variety of adaptations equip animals for survival in different environments. Lungs and gills, different in structure but similar in function, enable terrestrial and aquatic animals to secure the oxygen they need in different environments. The tearing teeth of a lion and the grinding teeth of a horse are both adapted to the food they eat. Among the most interesting adaptations for survival are those of form and color which render animals inconspicuous against the backgrounds of their normal habitats. Katydids and many other animals that live among leaves are typically green. Desert animals are often sandy in color and Arctic animals are often white. The flounder is remarkable in being able to change its color to conform to its background. This bottom-feeding fish turns pink, greenish or other colors and even becomes spotted in different ways so that it merges with the background.

flounder on sand (above)   flounder on stones (below)

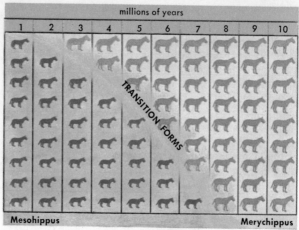

millions of years										
1	2	3	4	5	6	7	8	9	10

Mesohippus   Merychippus

each symbol = 1,000 horses

ADAPTATIONS AND EVOLUTION. Imagine sheep-sized horses defenseless except for their speed. Suppose, as a result of mutations, a colt should be born with longer, stronger legs, and capable of much greater speed. Beset by carnivores, the larger, fleeter animal would be more likely to live long enough to produce offspring. If its offspring were like itself they might produce descendants which would prosper, while the sheep sized horses might become extinct. Thus, the small, slower horse would have evolved into the larger, faster horse.

We know that such evolution did occur. The sheep-sized Mesohippus lived during the Oligocene. Ten million years later, in the Miocene, it was extinct, replaced by the pony-sized Merychippus. Fossils show that the one evolved into the other—not in one jump, but over millions of years. The chart depicts the extinction of Mesohippus and rise of Merychippus.

142

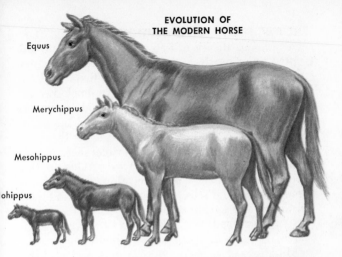

Equus

Merychippus

Mesohippus

ohippus

THE FACT OF EVOLUTION is incontrovertible. Fossils present documentation that modern forms of life evolved from earlier forms. The development of cat-sized horses and their further evolution into larger, fleeter animals occurred gradually over many millions of years. Above are four stages in the evolution of the horse (details of skulls and feet are shown on p. 10). From fossil remains of bones and teeth, comparable stages in the evolution of elephants, camels, monkeys and other animals have been reconstructed. Other evidences of the evolution of animals are found in their internal anatomy and embryonic development. Vestigial organs, like the human appendix and splint bones of modern horse (remnants of former toes) are found in all higher vertebrates and represent remnants of formerly useful structures. Mammals and birds go through stages with gill pouches (p. 144)—first like fish, then like reptiles.

THE MECHANISM OF EVOLUTION is complex. Darwin's famous theory of natural selection is still accepted by scientists, but it is not a total explanation of evolution. Darwin's theory states that: 1. Wide variation exists within and among animal species. 2. Animals tend to overproduce their kind, leading to competition for limited food, space and mates. 3. This endless competition creates a struggle for existence. 4. Because of variation—the differences in animals—some are better adapted to survive in this struggle than others. This survival of the fittest is a process of natural selection in which the less fit tend to die out and the fittest live to reproduce their kind. Darwin assumed that species of animals change slowly in response to changes in their environment.

Mutations of genes provide an explanation of the "how" of evolution. Darwin did not know how new variations were produced. DeVries, a Dutch botanist, later discovered that sudden, usually minor, changes or mutations (p. 139) in genes could be the source of these variations. Some mutations improve an animal's chances of survival. Over millions of years , enough advantageous mutations would occur to produce the gradual evolution of animals seen in the fossil record. There are other factors in evolution, but natural selection of variations produced by mutations seems to be the basic mechanism.

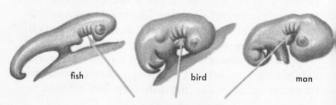

fish   bird   man

EMBRYONIC GILL POUCHES

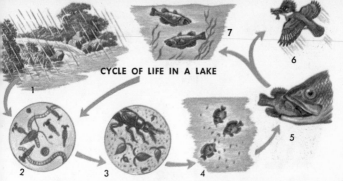

CYCLE OF LIFE IN A LAKE

Animals and Environments

An intricate interdependence of living things exists in all natural communities. The basic relationship between green plants and animals maintains a balance between carbon dioxide and oxygen in the atmosphere. This relationship also provides the basic energy in foods which all animals get, directly or indirectly, from plants. Minerals also go through cycles between and among plants and animals.

A greatly simplified account of these cycles is diagrammed above. (1) Rains wash nutrients into the lake. (2) Microscopic animals use these materials as food—plants use them in food manufacture. (3) Insects, insect larvae, and other tiny forms of life devour such plankton and each other. (4) Fingerling fish eat the algae, insects, larvae and so forth. (5) Larger fish prey upon smaller fish and, (6) terrestrial animals and birds eat the larger fish. But as large fish die, their bodies decompose into simple nutrients, (7) which are eaten by microscopic animals and used by plants. Thus the cycle begins again. A comparable forest community chain is shown on p. 146.

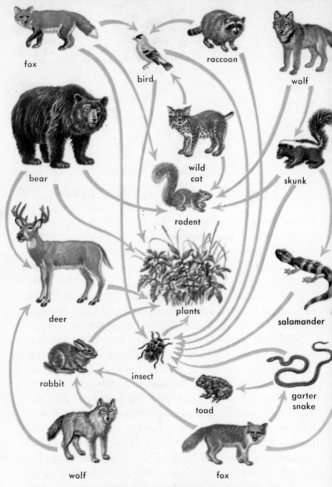

FOOD CHAIN IN A FOREST COMMUNITY
Arrows point from the eating animal to the animals or
plants that are eaten. This diagram is simplified—many
kinds of invertebrates and plants are also consumed.

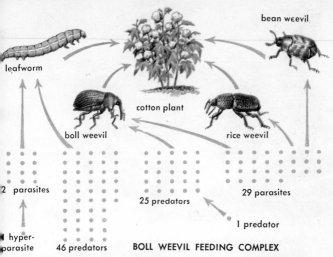

leafworm

bean weevil

cotton plant

boll weevil

rice weevil

2 parasites

25 predators

29 parasites

1 predator

hyper-
parasite

46 predators

BOLL WEEVIL FEEDING COMPLEX

PLANTS ARE BASIC LINK in food chains of both land and aquatic life. In the seas, diatoms and other algal plants manufacture food. They are eaten by protozoans and small crustaceans. These in turn are devoured by baby fish, which are eaten by small adult fish. These are eaten by still larger fish—and so forth. Death and decay of any of these organisms frees nitrogen for the algae and the chain is completed.

Actually, all such food chains are tremendously complex. Most animals are not only preyed upon by predators, they are also afflicted with parasites. And even the parasites themselves have parasites, or hyperparasites. The chart above is a simplified version of the "Boll Weevil Complex." Serving as food for a variety of insects, four of which are diagrammed, the cotton plant indirectly supports a host of other animals including hyperparasites.

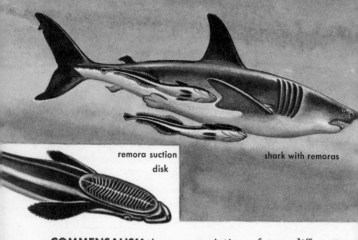

remora suction disk

shark with remoras

COMMENSALISM is an association of two different species in which one benefits and the other benefits little or not at all. But unlike what happens in parasitism, the host animal is not harmed. The remora or shark sucker has a sucker disk on its head. It attaches to sharks or other fish and takes a free ride. When the host feeds, the remora detaches, eats the scraps, then re-attaches and waits until the next meal.

sea anemone

Sea anemones, marine coelenterates (p. 30), live attached to rocks and piles. They sometimes attach themselves to the shells of hermit crabs. As the crabs move about in search of food the anemones are carried with them. Hence they have a better chance to get food than would be possible if they were fixed to one spot.

hermit crab

MUTUALISM is a relationship between two different species in which both benefit from the association. A classic example is shown below. Termites (p. 62) feed on wood, which is practically pure cellulose and which they can't digest. Investigation has disclosed a tremendous number of protozoa in the intestinal tracts of termites. These digest the cellulose and throw off waste products. These waste materials serve as the food supply of the termites. The protozoans, in turn, require the ground wood and intestinal environment of the termites. Each would die without the other. Mutualism also occurs between animals and plants. The flowers of yucca plants can be pollinated only by the yucca moth. Female moths lay eggs in the ovary wall, transferring pollen in the process. Larval moths feed on some of the developing seeds. Neither the plant nor the animal can exist one without the other.

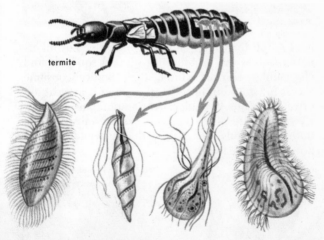

termite

protozoans from termite intestine

snowshoe rabbit in summer

snowshoe rabbit in winter

ADJUSTMENTS TO SEASONS are made by most animals. In the far north a seasonal molt gives many birds and mammals white winter coats. Winter creates food problems. Many birds and some bats migrate southward. Most insects spend the winter as inactive pupae or adults. Beavers and gophers store

geese migrating south

food in fall for winter eating. Winter sleep or hibernation solves the problem for ground squirrels and chipmunks. During winter, their bodies consume excess fat stored in fall. Breathing and heartbeat are extremely slow. In colder areas amphibians and reptiles hibernate also — under rocks or soil or at the bottom of ponds. Bears sleep during winter but are not true hibernators.

moth cocoon

chipmunk, hibernating

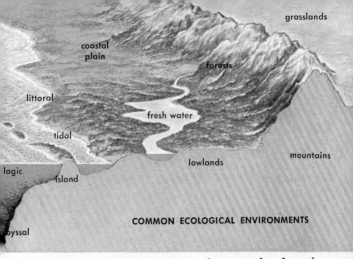

grasslands

coastal plain

forests

littoral

fresh water

tidal

lagic

mountains

island

lowlands

abyssal

COMMON ECOLOGICAL ENVIRONMENTS

ECOLOGICAL DISTRIBUTION refers to the broad kinds of environment in which animals are found. Some animals, like the harbor seal, are found in oceans nearly all over the world. But their ecological distribution is restricted to the shallow waters of the sea coasts. In general, similar species have a similar ecological distribution. Grass-eating herbivores, for example, are found in prairies all over the world. A desert or marsh in Asia is likely to have species of animals similar to those of a desert or marsh in North America or Africa. Ecological zoning also occurs vertically, as in oceans. Pelagic (upper level) sea life is different from middle level life, which in turn is different from life at abyssal depths. Similar vertical zoning occurs on mountain slopes.

The diagram above shows the major ecological zones of a continental margin but does not include important temperature-moisture zones such as deserts and tropical rain forests.

151

House wren
defending territory

TERRITORIALITY—"SQUATTER'S RIGHTS." Competition for food and living space often creates a kind of continuing warfare within a given species. The first pair of wrens to arrive at the nesting grounds in spring "stakes out" a territory and fights off other wrens attempting to invade it. If two wren houses are close, one is almost certain to remain untenanted because of the furious attacks of the first pair to reach the nesting site. Below is a typical pattern of nesting. Shrikes are particularly fierce in protecting their territory. Shrikes space themselves almost uniformly on telephone wires—each a fighting sovereign of its own hunting area.

house wren territories

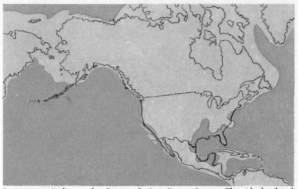

Green area indicates land mass during Cenozoic era. The Alaska land bridge enabled Asian animals to migrate to America.

ECOLOGICAL DISTRIBUTION AND BARRIERS. Both plants and animals in an area tend to produce more offspring than the environment can support. Living things tend, therefore, to spread out from their centers of origin. A species will spread out in all practical directions insofar as a suitable environment permits. But natural barriers restrict such movements. Bison of the North American plains, for example, could not move into South America because of the absence of grasslands in southern United States and northern Mexico. Oceans, mountain ranges and distinct differences in climate all create barriers and restrict animal ranges.

Present barriers did not always exist. North America, for example, was connected with Asia during most of the Cenozoic era. Horses and camels then moved from North America to Asia. Later, the land bridge sank and North America was once more isolated. Horses and camels became extinct in North America but continued their evolution in Eurasia.

China

Australia

Autralia was
once part of mainland.

platypus

GEOGRAPHICAL DISTRIBUTION of different species varies greatly. Some insects are found only on a particular plant growing only in one tract of a few acres. Beavers are found over much of North America and Europe. The housefly and rat are found over nearly all the habitable globe. The geographical distribution of any species constantly changes. Extensive droughts and disease may narrow the range. Man, clearing the land and planting crops, has reduced the range of some animals, such as the bison, but increased the range of others—such as foxes, quail, pheasants and opossums.

Vast geographical changes have occurred in the geological past. Australia was once a part of the Eurasian continent. In the millions of years since it was cut off from the mainland, animals evolved that are found nowhere else on earth. The mammals pictured here are found only in the Australian area.

spiny anteater

kangaroo

MAJOR ANIMAL REALMS today are shown on map and examples given in the table below. Each realm is characterized by certain native animals typical only of the area. The realms overlap slightly, the Palearctic and Nearctic having the most comparable forms. The Australian Realm has long been isolated. So the most distinctive animals are found there.

MAJOR ANIMAL REALMS

PALEARCTIC
Hedgehog, wild boar, fallow and roe deer.

ETHIOPIAN
African elephant, lion, zebra, hippopotamus, African rhinoceros, ostrich, giraffe, chimpanzee, gorilla

ORIENTAL
Indian elephant, Indian rhinoceros, jungle fowl, peacock, tarsier, macaque, gibbon, orangutan

AUSTRALIAN
Duck-bill platypus, spiny anteater, kangaroo and other marsupials—no native placental animals

NEARCTIC
Caribou, mountain goat, muskrat, prong-horned antelope

NEOTROPICAL
Armadillo, anteater, llama, alpaca, peccary, vampire bat, arboreal sloth, toucan

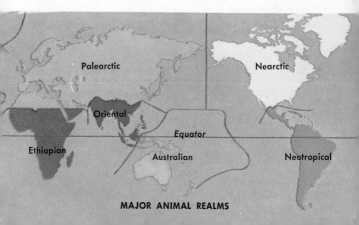

MAJOR ANIMAL REALMS

BOOKS FOR FURTHER STUDY

Nature Guides make study and identification of animals easier. The Golden Nature Guides contain hundreds of full-color paintings; text describes animals and how they live. See listing on book cover.

General Zoology Textbooks provide accurate, detailed information on the college level for serious amateurs or students. The following are among the better known and most readable:

STORER AND USINGER, *General Zoology*, McGraw-Hill, 1958. An outstanding and comprehensive book. Detailed and tightly written, requires and rewards careful reading.

ELLIOTT, ALFRED M., *Zoology*, Appleton-Century-Crofts, 1957. Interesting and readable.

Invertebrate Zoology Books of special merit are:

BUCHSBAUM, R., *Animals without Backbones*, Univ. of Chicago Press, 1948. Interesting, readable college text with outstanding pictures.

RICKETTS, E. F. AND C. J., *Between Pacific Tides*, Stanford Univ. Press, 1948. A guide that is more than a guide, this book is a readable account of Pacific tidal invertebrates.

Human Biology and Inheritance

CARLSON AND JOHNSON, *Machinery of the Body*, Univ. of Chicago Press, 1953. Authoritative and fascinating account of human structure and function. An outstanding and readable college text.

SCHEINFELD, AMRAM, *New You and Heredity*, Lippincott, 1950. A fascinating and clear treatment of human inheritance. Popular and accurate.

WINCHESTER, A. M., *Heredity and Your Life*, Vantage Press, 1956. Clearly and accurately written by a specialist.

Evolution

SIMPSON, GEORGE GAYLORD, *The Major Features of Evolution*, Columbia Univ. Press, 1953. Written by a leading authority.

SIMPSON, GEORGE GAYLORD, *The Meaning of Evolution*, Yale Univ. Press, 1950. A fascinating and important book.

Ecology

STORER, JOHN H., *The Web of Life*, Devin-Adair, 1953. A simple introduction to ecology.

BUCHSBAUM AND BUCHSBAUM, *Basic Ecology*, Boxwood Press, Pittsburgh, 1957. An excellent account of the science of ecology.

PLACES TO VISIT

Museums, zoos, aquaria and biological stations offer opportunities to extend your study of zoology—and don't forget that parks, fields, woods, streams, and even backyards teem with interesting animal life.

Museums of natural history are found at many universities and large cities. Here are some worth visiting:

Chicago: Chicago Natural History Museum.
Denver: Colorado Academy of Sciences.
Los Angeles: Los Angeles County Museum.
New York: American Museum of Natural History.
San Francisco: California Academy of Sciences.
Washington, D.C.: U.S. National Museum.

Zoos provide an opportunity to study a wide range of animals, often in natural habitats. Some major zoos are:

Chicago: Chicago Zoological Society, Brookfield Zoo.
Chicago: Lincoln Park Zoological Society.
Cincinnati: Cincinnati Zoological Gardens.
Miami: Cranden Park Zoo.
New York: New York Zoological Society, Bronx Park.
Philadelphia: Philadelphia Zoological Park.
Pittsburgh: Highland Park Zoo.
St. Louis: St. Louis Zoological Garden, Forest Park.
San Diego: San Diego Zoological Society, Balboa Park.
San Francisco: Fleisbaker Zoo.
Washington, D.C.: National Zoological Park.

Aquaria Some of the major one are:

Chicago: Shedd Aquarium.
Philadelphia: Fairmont Park Aquarium.
Marineland (near St. Augustine, Fla.): Marineland.
Miami: Seaquarium.
San Francisco: Steinhart Aquarium.
Washington, D.C.: U.S. Fish and Wildlife Aquarium.

Biological Stations carry on scientific studies and are of interest to serious amateurs. Mountain, desert, fresh water and other stations exist. List below is of major marine stations.

Marine Biological Laboratory, Woods Hole, Mass.
Oceanographic Inst., Fla. State Univ., Alligator Harbor, Fla.
Univ. of Miami Marine Laboratory, Miami, Fla.
Gulf Coast Research Laboratory, Ocean Springs, Miss.
Hopkins Marine Station, Pacific Grove, Cal.
Puget Sound Marine Biol. Station, Univ. of Wash., Friday Harbor, Wash.
Scripps Institution of Oceanography, La Jolla, Cal.

INDEX

Asterisks (*) indicate illustrations.

159